THINKING ABOUT STATUTES

Interpretation, Interaction, Improvement

We are in the age of statutes; and it is indisputable that statutes are swallowing up the common law. Yet the study of statutes as a coherent whole is rare. In these three lectures, given as the 2017 Hamlyn Lecture series, Professor Andrew Burrows takes on the challenge of thinking seriously and at a practical level about statutes in English law. In his characteristically lively and punchy style, he examines three central aspects which he labels interpretation, interaction and improvement. So how are statutes interpreted? Is statutory interpretation best understood as seeking to effect the intention of Parliament or is that an unhelpful fiction? Can the common law be developed by analogy to statutes? Do the judges have too much power in developing the common law and in interpreting statutes? How can our statutes be improved? These and many other questions are explored and answered in this accessible and thought-provoking analysis.

ANDREW BURROWS, QC (Hon), FBA, DCL, Barrister and Honorary Bencher of Middle Temple is Professor of the Law of England in the University of Oxford and a Fellow of All Souls College. He was a Law Commissioner for England and Wales (1994–1999) and President of the Society of Legal Scholars (2016–2017). His other books include *Remedies for Torts and Breach of Contract*, *The Law of Restitution*, *A Restatement of the English Law of Unjust Enrichment* and *A Restatement of the English Law of Contract*. He is a joint author of *Anson's Law of Contract*, the general editor of *English Private Law* and an editor of *Chitty on Contracts* and *Clerk and Lindsell on Torts*.

THE HAMLYN LECTURES 2017

THINKING ABOUT STATUTES

Interpretation, Interaction, Improvement

ANDREW BURROWS

CAMBRIDGE
UNIVERSITY PRESS

CAMBRIDGE
UNIVERSITY PRESS

University Printing House, Cambridge CB2 8BS, United Kingdom

One Liberty Plaza, 20th Floor, New York, NY 10006, USA

477 Williamstown Road, Port Melbourne, VIC 3207, Australia

314-321, 3rd Floor, Plot 3, Splendor Forum, Jasola District Centre, New Delhi - 110025, India

79 Anson Road, #06-04/06, Singapore 079906

Cambridge University Press is part of the University of Cambridge.

It furthers the University's mission by disseminating knowledge in the pursuit of
education, learning and research at the highest international levels of excellence.

www.cambridge.org
Information on this title: www.cambridge.org/9781108465786
DOI: 10.1017/9781108565981

First published 2018

A catalogue record for this publication is available from the British Library

Library of Congress Cataloging in Publication data
NAMES: Burrows, A. S. (Andrew S.), author.
TITLE: Thinking about statutes : interpretation, interaction, improvement / Andrew
Burrows, University of Oxford.
DESCRIPTION: Cambridge [UK] ; New York, NY : Cambridge University Press,
[2018] | Includes bibliographical references and index.
IDENTIFIERS: LCCN 2018015381 | ISBN 9781108475013 (alk. paper)
SUBJECTS: LCSH: Statutes – England. | Law – England – Interpretation and
construction.
CLASSIFICATION: LCC KD691 .B87 2018 | DDC 349.42–dc23
LC record available at https://lccn.loc.gov/2018015381

ISBN 978-1-108-47501-3 Hardback
ISBN 978-1-108-46578-6 Paperback

CONTENTS

The Hamlyn Trust owes its existence today to the will of the late Miss Emma Warburton Hamlyn of Torquay, who died in 1941 at the age of eighty. She came from an old and well-known Devon family. Her father, William Bussell Hamlyn, practised in Torquay as a solicitor and JP for many years, and it seems likely that Miss Hamlyn founded the trust in his memory. Emma Hamlyn was a woman of strong character, intelligent and cultured; well-versed in literature, music and art; and a lover of her country. She travelled extensively in Europe and Egypt, and apparently took considerable interest in the law, ethnology and culture of the countries that she visited. An account of Miss Hamlyn may be found, under the title 'The Hamlyn Legacy', in Volume 42 of the published lectures.

Miss Hamlyn bequeathed the residue of her estate on trust in terms which, it seems, were her own. The wording was thought to be vague, and the will was taken to the Chancery Division of the High Court which, in November 1948, approved a Scheme for the administration of the trust. Paragraph 3 of the Scheme, which follows Miss Hamlyn's own wording, is as follows:

> The object of the charity is the furtherance by lecturers or otherwise among the Common People of the United

Kingdom of Great Britain and Northern Ireland of the
knowledge of the Comparative Jurisprudence and
Ethnology of the Chief European countries including the
United Kingdom, and the circumstances of the growth of
such jurisprudence to the Intent that the Common People
of the United Kingdom may realise the privileges which in
law and custom they enjoy in comparison with other
European Peoples and realising and appreciating such
privileges may recognise the responsibilities and
obligations attaching to them.

The Trustees are to include the Vice-Chancellor of the University of Exeter; representatives of the Universities of London, Leeds, Glasgow, Belfast and Wales; and persons co-opted. At present, there are eight Trustees:

Professor Rosa Greaves, University of Glasgow
Ms Clare Dyer
Professor Chantal Stebbings (Chair, representing the Vice-
  Chancellor of the University of Exeter)
Professor R. Halson, University of Leeds
Professor J. Morison, Queen's University, Belfast
Sir Stephen Sedley
Professor A. Sherr, University of London
Professor Thomas Glyn Watkin, Bangor University

From the outset, it was decided that the objects of the Trust could be best achieved by means of an annual course of public lectures of outstanding interest and quality by eminent lecturers, and by their subsequent publication and distribution to a wider audience. The first of the Lectures was delivered by the Rt Hon. Lord Justice Denning (as he then was) in 1949. Since then, there has been an unbroken series of annual Lectures published until 2005 by Sweet & Maxwell and from 2006 by Cambridge University Press. A complete list of the Lectures may be found on pages ix to xiii. In 2005, the Trustees decided to supplement the Lectures with an annual Hamlyn Seminar, normally held at the Institute of Advanced Legal Studies at the University of London, to mark the publication of the Lectures in printed book form. The Trustees have also, from time to time, provided financial support for a variety of projects, which, in various ways, have disseminated knowledge or have promoted to a wider public understanding of the law.

This, the sixty-ninth series of Lectures, was delivered by Andrew Burrows at the University of Oxford, the University of Manchester and the Institute of Advanced Legal Studies, London. The Board of Trustees would like to record its appreciation to Andrew Burrows and also the three venues which generously hosted these Lectures.

CHANTAL STEBBINGS
Chair of the Trustees

Statutes are swallowing up our common law. Yet, despite their practical importance, statutes have never been the focus of a Hamlyn Lecture Series. In these three lectures, I have taken on the challenge of thinking seriously and at a practical level, and in a lively way, about statutes in English law by examining three central aspects, which, for shorthand, I label interpretation, interaction and improvement.

The first lecture on 'Statutory Interpretation' examines four main questions. What is the present English law on how a statute is to be interpreted? Is statutory interpretation best understood as seeking to effect the intention of Parliament or is that an unhelpful fiction? What insights are to be gained by the idea that a statute is 'always speaking'? And can we assimilate statutory interpretation with other types of legal interpretation, in particular the interpretation of contracts and common law precedents?

In a common law system, intriguing questions arise about the interaction between common law and statute. The second lecture on 'The Interaction of Common Law and Statute' examines three main issues concerned with that interaction. First, it looks at the development of the common law by analogy to statutes. Secondly, it explores the removal of the common law, or the freezing of its development, by statute. Thirdly, it considers the reform of the common law: should that be by judicial development or by statute?

The third lecture on 'Improving Statutes' asks how we might improve the quality of our statutes. Drawing on my experience as a Law Commissioner for England and Wales, a number of different avenues are explored. These include the style of statutory drafting, the role of Parliamentary Counsel, the work of the Law Commission in respect of consolidation and statute law repeals, and pre- and post-legislative scrutiny.

The main themes of the three lectures can be summarised as follows.

First, we need to spend far more time in our university law schools researching, and teaching in an engaging and practical way, about statute law as a coherent whole. Studying statutes as a coherent whole also helps us to understand properly the many fascinating issues raised by the interaction between common law and statute.

Secondly, in both the first and second lectures much of the focus is on the power of the judiciary as against the Legislature. While judicial law-making power through development of the common law has been widely recognised, the power of the judiciary in respect of statutory interpretation remains obfuscated by the idea that the courts are simply effecting the intention of Parliament. That idea tends to operate as a fiction or mask. It is unacceptable, as we strive for rational transparency, for the courts' true reasoning to be hidden in that way. At the same time, we should recognise that both in interpreting statutes and in developing the common law, the judges operate under institutional constraints, which render it misleading to think of them as unelected mini-legislators. In any event, in our system, Parliamentary sovereignty is the ultimate check on judicial power.

Thirdly, we have the statutes that we deserve. I have a vision of an up-to-date freely accessible electronic statute database with statutes that are as easy as possible to understand because the principles have been made clear and are enlivened by examples, have been subject to pre-legislative scrutiny, are consolidated where helpful, where there are no obsolete intruders, and where the lessons of the past have been learnt through systematic post-legislative scrutiny. But fulfilment of that vision requires both resources and education.

The printed lectures are slightly fuller versions of the lectures as I delivered them in November 2017. I have also taken the opportunity to make some light amendments throughout and have tried to deal with points raised after the lectures. It is hoped that the written version maintains the 'feel' of being at a lecture.

I would like to thank Lady Hale, President of the Supreme Court, for chairing Lecture 1 in Oxford; Lord Dyson, former Master of the Rolls and Supreme Court judge, for chairing Lecture 2 in Manchester; and Elizabeth Gardiner, First Parliamentary Counsel, for chairing Lecture 3 in London.

In relation to Lecture 1, I am grateful for discussions with Adrian Briggs, Justice James Edelman, Wolfgang Ernst, John Gardner and Fred Wilmot-Smith and for written comments from Richard Ekins. As regards Lecture 2, I am grateful for discussions with, and written comments from, Alison Young and for written comments from John Murphy. With respect to Lecture 3, I am grateful for

xvii

discussions with, and written comments from, Elizabeth Gardiner, First Parliamentary Counsel, and for discussions with Philip Davies, former Parliamentary Counsel, and Daniel Greenberg, Counsel for Domestic Legislation, House of Commons. I would also like to thank those Parliamentary Counsel who sent me emailed comments after Lecture 3. In relation to all three lectures, I found the question and answer session following each of the lectures very helpful and thank those who contributed.

I consider it an honour and a privilege to have been asked to deliver the Hamlyn Lectures 2017. I thank the Hamlyn trustees for inviting me and especially Chantal Stebbings, chair of the trustees, and Sir Stephen Sedley, for their support and help throughout.

TABLE OF STATUTES

xxvi

Lecture 1

Statutory Interpretation

In the famous words of Professor Guido Calabresi, we are 'in the age of statutes';[1] and it is indisputable that statutes are swallowing up our common law. Yet oddly, although they have been touched on, statutes have never been the focus of a Hamlyn Lecture Series. Perhaps this reflects their status in UK legal academia where the study of statutes as a coherent whole is sadly neglected, especially by those specialising in private law like me. While particular statutes or statutory provisions within a particular area of substantive law (e.g. contract law or tort law or employment law or company law) are studied, albeit generally without much enthusiasm compared to the common law, statute law as a coherent whole tends to be treated only at a basic introductory level in, for example, first year English Legal System or Legal Skills courses.[2] Even where statute law as a whole is taken more seriously, this is often either at

---

[1] Guido Calabresi, *A Common Law for the Age of Statutes* (Harvard University Press, 1982) at 181.

[2] *Teaching Legislation in UK Law Schools : Summary of Survey Results* (2011) (carried out for the Statute Law Society by Professor Stefan Voganauer and accessible at www.statutelawsociety.co.uk/library for 2012) showed that in only 19% of UK law schools (who responded to the survey, there being a response rate of 47.04%) was there a dedicated course or teaching unit on legislation; and 56% of such courses were for first years.

a theoretical level in jurisprudence courses or as a relatively small part of the constitutional law syllabus. As Lord Steyn has said, '[T]he academic profession and universities have not entirely caught up with the reality that statute law is the dominant source of law of our time.'[3] And in the words of Professor Neil Duxbury, 'Generally speaking, statute law has been regarded as a dusty and uninviting academic topic – in so far as it has been considered an academic topic at all.'[4]

In these three lectures, I want to rise to the challenge of thinking seriously, and at a practical level, about statutes by examining three central aspects, which, for shorthand, I label interpretation, interaction and improvement. So, in this first lecture, I am looking at statutory interpretation.

I should stress at the outset that my focus in these lectures is on statutes – on primary legislation, that is Acts of Parliament[5] – and not on secondary or delegated legislation contained in, for example, statutory instruments. Although

---

[3] Johan Steyn, 'The Intractable Problem of the Interpretation of Legal Texts' (2003) 25 *Sydney Law Review*, 5.

[4] Neil Duxbury, *Elements of Legislation* (Cambridge, 2013) at 64.

[5] I confine myself to what are termed 'public general Acts'. There is a small but declining number of Acts each year that are termed 'local Acts'. Albeit that we might still say they are passed in the public interest, such local Acts are confined in scope to a limited area or a limited class of people (i.e. they may be local or personal). As regards statutory interpretation, it would appear that local Acts are interpreted in the same way as public general Acts, although there has been an occasional reference to a rule of *contra proferentem* operating against the promoters of a local Act. See generally Daniel Greenberg, *Craies on Legislation* (11th edn, Sweet & Maxwell, 2017) paras. 1.4.1–1.4.11; 29.1.12. I am also dealing with Acts of Parliament only and not with legislation of the Northern Irish Assembly, the National Assembly for Wales or the Scottish Parliament.

almost all of what I shall say is equally applicable to secondary legislation, I put to one side any distinct issues that may arise in relation to secondary legislation. So, for example, although a topic of great importance that has been brought into sharp focus by Brexit, I shall not be dealing with the divide between primary and secondary legislation and the use of so-called Henry VIII clauses.[6]

I have divided this first lecture into four parts. First, I want to give an overview of the modern approach in English law to statutory interpretation. Secondly, I want to consider the extent to which, if at all, statutory interpretation is best seen as effecting the intention of Parliament. Thirdly, I want to focus on the idea that a statute is 'always speaking'. Fourthly, I want to compare and contrast statutory interpretation with some other forms of legal interpretation.

1 What Is the Present English Law on Statutory Interpretation?

Before answering this, it should be stressed just how important, in the practice of law, statutory interpretation has become. As Justice Kirby, formerly of the High Court of Australia, has said, '[T]he construction of statutes is now, probably, the single most important aspect of legal and judicial work ... This is what I, and every other judge in the countries of the world that observe the rule of law, spend most

---

[6] In general terms, these clauses give Ministers the power in secondary legislation to amend primary legislation. See Lecture 3, note 8.

of our time doing.'[7] Yet in line with the general neglect of statutes in our law school curricula, statutory interpretation is rarely given the attention it merits. As Lord Justice Sales said in his address to the Society of Legal Scholars in Oxford in 2016, 'Most of the law which the courts are called on to apply is statutory. Yet statutory interpretation languishes as a subject of study. For the most part, law students are expected to pick it up by a sort of process of osmosis.'[8] It follows that, if I were to ask this audience tonight, 'What are the leading cases on statutory interpretation?', I suspect that, with the exception of *Pepper* v. *Hart*,[9] I would be met either with a blank or with a myriad of different cases dealing with different specific statutes. I would also hazard a guess that it would not be long before someone referred to the literal rule, the mischief rule and the golden rule. These rules have often been trotted out in basic textbook treatments – I remember that I first came across them when reading Glanville Williams' introductory book *Learning the Law*[10] before I came to university – but they cast very little light on the modern approach. Indeed, we may ask: where did that analysis or categorisation of the rules on statutory interpretation come from? We do not find them neatly set out and labelled in that way in any case. The answer is that they come from a relatively little known article – this must be the most referred to and yet least properly cited

---

[7] The Hon Michael Kirby, 'Towards a Grand Theory of Interpretation: The Case of Statutes and Contracts' (2002) 24 *Statute Law Review* 95, 96–97.

[8] Lord Justice Sales, 'Modern Statutory Interpretation' (2017) 38 *Statute Law Review* 125, 125.

[9] [1993] AC 593. [10] (ed. A.T.H. Smith, 16th edn, Sweet & Maxwell, 2016).

article of all time – entitled 'Statutory Interpretation in a Nutshell' appearing in the 1938 *Canadian Bar Review* and written by a Canadian academic Professor John Willis.[11]

Certainly, it is not easy to pin down the present approach of the courts. Although said in 1956, the words of Lord Evershed MR remain accurate today: '[S]ome judicial utterance can be cited in support of almost any proposition relevant to the problems of statutory interpretation.'[12]

However, it is tolerably clear today that our judges have moved from an old literal to a modern contextual and purposive approach. We no longer gives words their literal or dictionary meaning in so far as the context and purpose of the statute indicate that that is not the best interpretation of what Parliament has enacted.[13] In *IRC* v. *McGuckian*[14] in 1997 Lord

---

[11] (1938) 16 *Canadian Bar Review*, 1. As explained by Willis, the 'literal rule' is that the words should be given their ordinary or plain meaning; the 'golden rule' is that the plain meaning of the words may be departed from to avoid absurdity (see *Grey* v. *Pearson* (1857) 6 HLC 61 at 106); and the 'mischief rule' is that the words should be interpreted to remedy the problem addressed by the statute (see *Heydon's Case* (1584) 3 Co Rep 7a; 76 ER 637).

[12] 'The Impact of Statute on the Law of England', Maccabean Lecture in Jurisprudence (1956) XLII *Proceedings of the British Academy* 247 at 258.

[13] In Australia, a purposive approach is laid down in statutes. So, e.g., s. 15AA of the (Commonwealth) Acts Interpretation Act 1901 (as amended) reads: 'In interpreting a provision of an Act, the interpretation that would best achieve the purpose or object of the Act . . . is to be preferred to each other interpretation.'

[14] [1997] 1 WLR 991 at 999. For other tax cases in which it was similarly stressed that the modern purposive interpretation applies even to tax statutes (contrary to a view that such statutes should continue to be interpreted applying the old literal approach) see: *Barclays Mercantile*

Steyn said: 'During the last 30 years, there has been a shift away from the literalist approach to purposive methods of construction ... the modern emphasis is on a contextual approach designed to identify the purpose of a statute and to give effect to it.' In Lord Bingham's words in *R v. Secretary of State for Health, ex p Quintavalle*, 'The court's task, within the permissible bounds of interpretation, is to give effect to Parliament's purpose. So the controversial provisions should be read in the context of the statute as a whole, and the statute as a whole should be read in the historical context of the situation which led to its enactment.'[15] In the same case, Lord Steyn again emphasised that a purposive, rather than a literal, approach was now to be taken. 'The pendulum has swung towards purposive methods of construction. This change was not initiated by the teleological approach of the European Community jurisprudence, and the influence of European legal culture generally, but it has been accelerated by European ideas ... [N]owadays the shift towards purposive interpretation is not in doubt.'[16] Lord Nicholls in *R v. Sec of State for the Environment, Transport and the Regions, ex p Spath Holme Ltd*[17] emphasised the importance of context saying, 'Statutory interpretation is an exercise which requires the court to identify the meaning borne by the words in question in the particular context.' And in the precisely accurate and succinct words of the late and sadly missed Toulson LJ, as he

Business Finance Ltd v. *Mawson* [2004] UKHL 51, [2005] 1 AC 684; *UBS AG* v. *HMRC* [2016] UKSC 13, [2016] 1 WLR 1005; *RFC 2012 Plc* v. *Advocate General for Scotland* [2017] UKSC 45, [2017] 1 WLR 2767.

[15] [2003] UKHL 13, [2003] 2 AC 687, at [8].   [16] Ibid. at [21].
[17] [2001] 2 AC 349, 397.

then was, in *An Informer* v. *A Chief Constable*, 'Construction of a phrase in a statute does not simply involve transposing a dictionary definition of each word. The phrase has to be construed according to its context and the underlying purpose of the provision.'[18]

Three specific points on the modern approach are noteworthy. First, the modern approach has subsumed many of the old so-called 'canons' of interpretation, such as the rule *eiusdem generis*[19] or the rule *expressio unius*[20] or, to

---

[18] [2012] EWCA Civ 197, [2013] QB 579 at [67]. See also for mention of both context and purpose Lord Nicholls in *MD Foods (formerly Associated Dairies) Ltd* v. *Baines* [1997] AC 524, 532: 'In the process of statutory interpretation there always comes a stage, before reaching a final decision, when one should stand back and view a suggested interpretation in the wider context of the scheme and purpose of the Act.' For the emphasis on purpose, see, e.g., Lords Griffiths and Browne-Wilkinson in *Pepper* v. *Hart* [1993] AC 593, 617, 633–634; and *Harrods Ltd* v. *Remick* [1998] 1 All ER 52, 58, where Scott LJ said, '[W]e should, in my judgment, give a construction to the statutory language that is not only consistent with the actual words used but also would achieve the statutory purpose of providing a remedy to victims of discrimination who would otherwise be without one.' In the same context of discrimination law, see *MHC Consulting Services Ltd* v. *Tansell* [2000] ICR 789, 798 (per Mummery LJ). For a compelling application of what he termed 'purposive considerations' so as to give a meaning to words that were linguistically possible even though not the most natural interpretation, see Henderson J in *Investment Trust Companies* v. *HMRC* [2012] EWHC 458 (Ch) at [104]–[105](decision on this upheld by the Supreme Court, also adopting a purposive construction [2017] UKSC 29, [2017] 2 WLR 1200, esp. at [80]).

[19] The meaning of this is that general words, following specific words, should be confined to things 'of the same kind'.

[20] The meaning of this is that where 'one thing is expressly mentioned', this is to the exclusion of others.

choose one not expressed in Latin, the rule that the scope of a criminal statute should be narrowly construed. While no doubt these canons or rules will continue to reflect what will usually be the best interpretation, they have lost primacy with the demise of literalism and have tended to be swallowed up by the modern contextual and purposive approach.[21] Secondly, much of the legislative history is now admissible (e.g. Law Commission Reports and White Papers and Explanatory Notes) and this includes, exceptionally and subject to constraints, Parliamentary debates from Hansard following the landmark case of *Pepper* v. *Hart*. Thirdly, in *Inco Europe Ltd* v. *First Choice Distribution*,[22] the House of Lords accepted that, very exceptionally, provided it is clear there has been a drafting mistake and it is clear what the statute was meant to say, the courts can amend the words of a statute. This has been labelled 'rectifying construction' or even just 'rectification'.

In understanding the move that the courts have made, it may be helpful to look at a couple of cases that epitomise the old literal approach. In doing so, I am conscious that there have been traces of a contextual and purposive

---

[21] *Karpavicius* v. *The Queen* [2002] UKPC 59, [2003] 1 WLR 169, at [15] (per Lord Steyn). See also *R (on the application of Black)* v. *Secretary of State for Justice* [2017] UKSC 81, [2018] AC 215. In this latter case, it was decided that the 'no smoking in public places' legislation does not apply to (state) prisons. But in relation to the long-standing presumption (or rebuttable rule) that the Crown is not bound by a statute, Lady Hale (giving the sole judgment) at [37] said, 'The question is whether, in the light of the words used, their context and the purpose of the legislation, Parliament must have meant the Crown to be bound.'

[22] [2000] 1 WLR 586.

approach throughout, going back to identifying the relevant 'mischief' being cured in *Heydon's Case* in 1584,[23] so that some would argue that the modern move is not as clear-cut as I have indicated[24] and that the literal approach I am about to illustrate was not adopted by all judges. Nevertheless, the two cases I am about to discuss, both from the 1960s, were decided as they were and would, in my view, clearly be decided differently today.

In *Fisher* v. *Bell*[25] the defendant was charged with the offence of 'offering for sale' a flick knife contrary to section 1(1) of the Restriction of Offensive Weapons Act 1959. He had displayed a flick knife in his shop window with a ticket behind it saying 'Ejector knife – 4s'. He was held to be not guilty because according to the Divisional Court, applying the words literally in the light of the principles of contract law, the display was not an offer to sell but rather a mere invitation to treat. The offer was made by the customer to buy the knife and there was therefore no offer to sell by the shopkeeper. Although this interpretation was in conflict with the purpose of the Act – as Lord Parker CJ said 'it sounds absurd that knives of this sort cannot be manufactured, sold, hired, or given, but apparently can be displayed in shop windows'[26] – that was a matter for the Legislature, not the courts, to sort out.

---

[23] (1584) 3 Co Rep 7a; 76 ER 637.

[24] See, e.g., Daniel Greenberg, 'All Trains Stop at Crewe: The Rise and Rise of Contextual Drafting' (2005) 7 *European Journal of Law Reform* 31; Daniel Greenberg, *Craies on Legislation* (11th edn, Sweet & Maxwell, 2017) ch. 18.

[25] [1961] 1 QB 394.   [26] Ibid. at 399–400.

In *Bourne* v. *Norwich Crematorium Ltd*[27] the claimant ran a crematorium and sought a statutory tax allowance for expenses in improving the furnace chamber and chimney of the crematorium. The allowance was applicable if the business could be said to be concerned with the 'subjection of goods or materials to any process'. The court held that those words did not cover the business of a crematorium because 'it is a distortion of the English language to describe the living or the dead as goods or materials'.[28] I would suggest that applying a modern purposive approach, a different result would now be reached. However, to avoid misunderstanding, it is crucial to clarify that the modern purposive approach does not mean that the words used in the statute can be ignored. On the contrary, the words used are of central importance so that the courts cannot depart from a plausible meaning of those words. There is a difference between, on the one hand, the literal meaning of words irrespective of context and purpose and, on the other hand, the best plausible meaning of the words in the light of their context and purpose. The courts have moved to adopting the latter approach. In the *Bourne* case, a literal meaning of the 'subjection of goods or materials to any process' did not embrace the business of a crematorium. But those words could plausibly embrace the business of a crematorium and that that was the best

---

[27] [1967] 1 WLR 691.

[28] Ibid. at 695 (per Stamp J). For criticism of Stamp J for taking a literal approach, see *The Interpretation of Statutes*, Law Commission Report No 21 (1969) para. 8. But while I agree that Stamp J is best understood as taking a literal approach, it is noteworthy that he did expressly recognise that context is important.

interpretation emerges clearly when we take into account the statutory context and purpose. The statutory tax allowance would clearly have applied, for example, to a business using a furnace chamber and chimney to dispose of waste material; and a plausible meaning of 'materials' includes corpses inside coffins. I return later to the significance of accepting that a constraint on the courts is that their interpretation must be a plausible (albeit not the literal) meaning of the words used.[29]

Everything that I have so far been talking about might be described as ordinary statutory interpretation. But in seeing the full picture on statutory interpretation, we should recognise the importance of non-standard interpretation, which for shorthand we can refer to as 'conforming interpretation'.[30] What I principally have in mind is the requirement under section 3 of the Human Rights Act 1998 that a statute (or indeed secondary legislation) should, so far as possible, be read in a way which is compatible with rights under the ECHR. A somewhat similar approach may also be seen as underpinning the *Marleasing* case,[31] which, until Brexit day, requires that a statute should, if at all possible, be

---

[29] See below at pp. 42–43.

[30] For use of that terminology, see, e.g., *R (IDT Card Services Ireland Ltd)* v. *HMRC* [2006] EWCA Civ 29, [2006] STC 1252, at [73]–[92] (Arden LJ).

[31] *Marleasing SA* v. *La Comercial Internacional de Alimentacion SA* [1990] ECR 1–4135, Case C-106/89. For the leading English case applying this principle, albeit prior to *Marleasing*, see *Litster* v. *Forth Dry Dock & Engineering Co Ltd* [1990] 1 AC 546. See also, e.g., *R (IDT Card Services Ireland Ltd)* v. *HMRC* [2006] EWCA Civ 29, [2006] STC 1252, at [73]–[92] (Arden LJ linking s. 3 of the Human Rights Act 1998 and *Marleasing*).

read as conforming to any relevant EU law.[32] This idea of conforming interpretation may further be regarded as embracing the 'principle of legality'[33] – that a statute should be read down to avoid the removal of fundamental common law or constitutional rights – which I will look at in my next lecture on the interaction of common law and statute.

As regards section 3 of the 1998 Act, the important point is that this requires a court to go beyond normal purposive and contextual interpretation to ensure, if possible, that the statute is compatible with convention rights. If necessary, a court must strain the meaning of the words used, and even omit or insert words, so as to ensure compatibility. Although section 3 is headed 'Interpretation of legislation', we can debate whether the section requires the courts to cross over from interpretation into statutory amendment. Even assuming that the task is always one of interpretation, it is clear that section 3 embraces the extreme end of the spectrum of the interpretative exercise and for that reason is controversial. Where the decision involves a controversial issue of social policy,[34] we would expect the courts to tread especially carefully, even though the power under

---

[32] A similar idea is the principle that statutes, at least if ambiguous, should be read as complying with the UK's treaty obligations: *Salomon* v. *Customs and Excise Commrs* [1967] 2 QB 116, 143–144; *JH Rayner Ltd* v. *Department of Trade and Industry* [1990] 2 AC 418; *Assuranceforeningen Gard Gjensidig* v. *The International Oil Pollution Compensation Fund* [2014] EWHC 1394 (Comm), [2014] 2 Lloyd's Rep 219.

[33] See, e.g., Sir Philip Sales, 'A Comparison of the Principle of Legality and Section 3 of the Human Rights Act 1998' (2009) 125 *Law Quarterly Review* 598. See below, pp. 68–74.

[34] See below, pp. 74–85, esp. at footnote 92.

section 3 is one that Parliament has explicitly conferred on them. The seminal example of its application was the decision of the House of Lords in *Ghaidan* v. *Godin-Mendoza*.[35] The question here was whether living 'as his or her wife or husband' under the Rent Act 1977, governing the survivorship of a statutory tenancy, included same-sex partners. Prior to the Human Rights Act 1998, in *Fitzpatrick* v. *Sterling Housing Association Ltd*[36] the House of Lords, applying a purposive and contextual approach, had held that while same-sex partners were members of a 'family' in respect of the survivorship of an *assured* tenancy, they could not be interpreted as living 'as his or her wife or husband' in respect of the survivorship of a *statutory* tenancy. That would conflict with the need for an opposite sex relationship, which was dictated by the words 'wife or husband'. However, after the enactment of the 1998 Act in *Ghaidan*, the House of Lords held that those words should be read as including same-sex partners. This ensured conformity with convention rights under Articles 8 and 14, and reading the words in that way was possible in the sense that that meaning went with 'the grain of the legislation'.[37]

2 Is Statutory Interpretation Seeking to Effect the Intention of Parliament?

It has historically been very common, and remains so, to refer to statutory interpretation as being concerned to effect the

---

[35] [2004] UKHL 30, [2004] 2 AC 557. See also, e.g., *McDonald* v. *McDonald* [2016] UKSC 28, [2017] AC 273.

[36] [2001] 1 AC 27.

[37] [2004] UKHL 30, [2004] 2 AC 557, at [121] (per Lord Rodger).

intention of Parliament. Whether applying the old literal or the modern contextual and purposive approach, the cases are full of references to this being the ultimate aim and most of us will have used this language.

Just to give one recent judicial example of it: in 2016 in *Campbell* v. *Peter Gordon Joiners Ltd*,[38] the question facing the Supreme Court was whether there was a tort action for breach of statutory duty by the employer and director of a company in failing to insure an employee contrary to the Employers' Liability (Compulsory Insurance) Act 1969. The Supreme Court held three to two that there was no such tort action. My own view is that the dissenting judgments of Lord Toulson and Lady Hale are to be preferred. However, it is noteworthy that, in orthodox fashion, Lady Hale's judgment is formulated in terms of a search for Parliament's intention. So in her words:

> The question for this court is whether in 1969, when Parliament passed sections 1 and 5 of the Employers' Liability (Compulsory Insurance) Act, it was intended that breach of those sections should give rise, not only to criminal liability, but also to civil liability towards an employee who had been injured by the employer's breach of duty towards him and who, because of the failure to insure, would otherwise not receive the compensation for his injuries to which he was entitled. In my view, it is absolutely plain that Parliament *did* intend there to be such civil liability.[39]

What exactly does such a reference to Parliamentary intention mean and is it a helpful concept at all?

[38] [2016] UKSC 38, [2016] AC 1513.   [39] Ibid. at [43].

Plainly, it cannot mean that we should be looking at the actual subjective intentions of all those involved – the Minister, the MPs, the Lords, the drafters, the bill team – because those intentions cannot be practically ascertained, and, in any event, they are most unlikely to coincide other than at a very general and unhelpful level. Three possibilities then present themselves.

First, we might say that the intention in question is objective not subjective, although this in turn raises questions as to what we mean here by 'objective'. So, for example, in *R v. Sec of State for the Environment, Transport and the Regions, ex parte Spath Holme Ltd*, Lord Nicholls said:

> '[T]he intention of Parliament' is an objective concept, not subjective. The phrase is a shorthand reference to the intention which the court reasonably imputes to Parliament in respect of the language used. It is not the subjective intention of the minister or other persons who promoted the legislation. Nor is it the subjective intention of the draftsman, or of individual members or even of a majority of individual members of either House. These individuals will often have widely varying intentions.[40]

Similarly, but with a particular emphasis on the understanding of the reasonable reader, Lord Hoffmann in *R (Wilkinson)*

[40] Lord Nicholls [2001] 2 AC 349, 397. Once it was realised the intention was objective and not subjective, his Lordship thought reference to Parliament's intention was 'correct and may be helpful'. See also Lord Nicholls, 'My Kingdom for a Horse: The Meaning of Words' (2005) 121 *Law Quarterly Review* 577, 589: 'As with the interpretation of contracts, courts apply an objective approach to the interpretation of Acts of Parliament.'

v. *IRC* said that: 'by the intention of Parliament ... [o]ne means the interpretation which the reasonable reader would give to the statute read against its background'.[41]

Secondly, there is the view, put forward in its most sophisticated form by Dr Richard Ekins in his 2012 book *The Nature of Legislative Intent*, that 'group theory' explains what is meant by Parliamentary intention. According to this view, it is perfectly natural to recognise the intentions of a group as a rational agent (so, to take a simple example, we say 'the intention of the team is to play attacking football'), and that this does not involve aggregating the intentions of individuals or picking out the intentions of certain leading individuals.[42] The Legislature is a complex group and what is

---

[41] [2005] UKHL 30, [2006] 1 All ER 529 at [18]. See also his judgment in *Att-Gen of Belize* v. *Belize Telecom Ltd* [2009] UKPC 10, [2009] 1 WLR 1988 at [16].

[42] Although in chapter 3 of his book, *The Nature of Legislative Intent* (Oxford, 2012) Ekins refers to a company as a group, he does not deal specifically with the legal approach to companies where, traditionally, the company's state of mind has been ascertained by looking at those who constitute the 'directing mind and will' of the company (although in the influential analysis of Lord Hoffmann, giving the judgment of the Privy Council, in *Meridian Global Funds Management Asia Ltd* v. *Securities Commission* [1995] 2 AC 500, it was stressed that all ultimately depends on the context in which the attribution question arises). This approach to companies contrasts with the approach to the intention of the Legislature where there is no equivalent attempt to ascertain the intention of leading legislators. Note also that the law on attribution in relation to companies has been developed so as to ensure that laws apply to companies; but there is no need to formulate attribution rules for the Legislature because the Legislature is not a legal person.

meant by legislative intention is that Parliament as a group acts with a rational plan, with linked procedures, to change the law in some way. So in Dr Ekins' view, it is a mistake to argue that any fiction is involved in perpetuating the long-standing tradition of referring to the intention of the Legislature.

A third view is that referring to the intention of Parliament is an unhelpful fiction or mask that should be avoided altogether. Intention, it can be argued, is here being used as a conclusion for a decision as to what a statute means that is reached on other grounds which should be openly recognised. So, for example,[43] Justice Kirby writing in 2002 said, '[I]t is unfortunately still common to see reference ... to the "intention of Parliament". I never use that expression now. It is potentially misleading.'[44] And Sir John Laws takes a similar view. In his *Law Quarterly Review* of Dr Ekins' book, he writes: 'The notion of intention ... denotes a conscious state of mind whereby ... [a] person proposes to act in a particular way. Since it denotes a state of mind, which is a characteristic of a single person, it cannot be possessed by a group, or an institution.'[45] And it is of course trite law that

[43] For sophisticated jurisprudential rejections of legislative intention, see, e.g., Ronald Dworkin, *Law's Empire* (Harvard University Press, 1986) 313–354; Jeremy Waldron, *Law and Disagreement* (Oxford, 1999) 119–146.

[44] Justice Michael Kirby, 'Towards a Grand Theory of Interpretation: The Case of Statutes and Contracts' (2002) *Statute Law Review* 95, 98.

[45] Review at (2016) 132 *Law Quarterly Review* 159. See also Sir John Laws, 'Statutory Interpretation – the Myth of Parliamentary Intent', Renton Lecture 13 November 2017 (which was delivered shortly after this Hamlyn Lecture and has since been made available on the website of the Statute Law Society). For a very supportive review of Ekins' book, see

the Legislature, unlike a company, is not treated as a legal person with capacity.[46] It is important to add, however, that Sir John Laws accepts that we can refer to the purpose, rather than the intention, of the Legislature. He therefore welcomes the modern movement to purposive interpretation but does not see that as helpfully underpinned by reference to Parliamentary intention.

My own preference is for the third of these views whereby we avoid all reference to Parliamentary intention. While speaking of Parliamentary intention may be said to remind the courts of the need to avoid crossing the important constitutional line between interpreting and legislating, and in that sense it is a constant reminder of the separation of powers, it can too easily become a mask for judges to hide their true reasoning. Dressing a decision up as effecting Parliamentary intention may divert attention away from scrutinising the judges – just as did the old fairy tale[47] that the judges discover and do not make the common law – and merely serves to obscure the power the judges are exercising in their interpretative role. Transparency dictates that the judges' true reasoning is not obfuscated by hiding away behind a fiction or mask, but is brought out into the open and scrutinised for what it is.

Even if we were to accept that Dr Ekins is providing a valid explanation for the traditional reliance on

Jeffrey Goldsworthy, 'Legislative Intention Vindicated?' (2013) 33 *Oxford Journal of Legal Studies* 821.

[46] Cf. local government, which is an incorporated body that has capacity, e.g., to enter into contracts.

[47] Brilliantly denounced as such by Lord Reid, 'The Judge as Lawmaker' (1972) 12 *Journal of the Society of Public Teachers of Law* (UK) 22.

Parliamentary intention, it is clear that the explanation provides no assistance at a practical level in answering the questions on statutory interpretation that the courts face. In other words, to say that Parliamentary intention means Parliament as a 'group' intends to change the law in some way by following the rules and procedures required in passing a statute is to say nothing more than that Parliament has validly passed a particular statute so that the statute is law; and plainly such a banal statement does not help the courts in deciding a dispute on statutory interpretation. In deciding on the best interpretation of a statute, the courts need to rely on the more concretised ideas that revolve around the words, context and purpose of the statute. Reliance on the 'high-level' idea of Parliamentary intention is unhelpful, at best, and has a tendency to mask the true reasoning and power of the courts.

Is it consistent to reject Parliamentary intention, while accepting 'purposive' interpretation as, for example, Sir John Laws has done? Although Ekins and others[48] have argued that this approach is inconsistent and draws a distinction without a difference, I do not agree. When we talk of 'purpose', we are looking for the policy behind the statute or statutory provision. Identifying the policy is not dependent on identifying any person's intentions. It may be said to be analogous to identifying the principle behind a common law precedent and that, too, is not dependent on

---

[48] See, e.g., Richard Ekins and Jeffrey Goldsworthy, 'The Reality and Indispensability of Legislative Intentions' (2014) 36 *Sydney Law Review* 39, 57.

trying to identify any person's (i.e. judge's) intention. Indeed to expose the practical irrelevance[49] of the legislator's intention, it may be helpful to focus on the statute, rather than the legislator, and to say that we are concerned with the meaning of the statute, ascertained by considering *the statute's* words, context and purpose.[50] Certainly, an advantage of such a switch of focus is that it helps to clarify that what ultimately matters is the judicial analysis, at the time a dispute arises, of what the statute means.

It follows that what Lady Hale really meant in *Campbell* v. *Peter Gordon Joiners Ltd* when she said that Parliament *did* intend there to be civil liability for breach of the statute is that a plausible meaning of the statutory words was that they imposed civil liability and there were convincing reasons, in achieving the statute's purpose, why there should be civil liability, even though the question of civil liability may never have crossed the minds of anyone in Parliament. Very importantly, Lady Hale did not ultimately hide behind the fiction of Parliamentary intention but went on to articulate with rational clarity what those convincing reasons were.

However, there may be more than just transparency of reasoning that is at stake here. Reference to the intention of

---

[49] As has been argued in the last paragraph, even if it were correct that, at a high level, there is a link between intention and purpose, at a practical level it is the purpose that matters.

[50] There is a clear distinction between the meaning of words and what the author intended those words to mean. And as French CJ said in 'Bending Words: The Fine Art of Interpretation' (University of Western Australia, 20 March 2014): 'One may discern a purpose for a constructed thing such as a tool without having to inquire about the intention of the maker.'

Parliament easily leads to the fundamental error of treating the judges' interpretative role as in some sense frozen at the time the legislation was enacted. This undermines the vital role that the judges have of interpreting legislation with the benefit of hindsight. The hindsight in question may not only be the facts of the particular dispute – it is always easier to ascribe meaning when we have the facts of a dispute to resolve – but crucially includes unforeseen changes that have occurred since the legislation was enacted. I now therefore want to turn, in the third part of this lecture, to the important insights for our understanding of statutory interpretation that can be gleaned from cases dealing with the idea that a statute is 'always speaking'.

3 A Statute Is 'Always Speaking'

It is trite law that, at least in general, a statute is 'always speaking' or, as it has otherwise been expressed, has an 'ambulatory meaning'.[51] Although what this precisely means is open to

---

[51] Apart from the cases mentioned below, see, e.g., *Fitzpartick* v. *Sterling Housing Association Ltd* [1999] 3 WLR 1113 (gay partner held to be a member of the 'family'); *R (Smeaton)* v. *Sec of State for Health* [2002] EWHC 610 (Admin) ('miscarriage'); *Re McFarland (AP) (Northern Ireland)* [2004] UKHL 17, [2004] 1 WLR 1289, per Lord Steyn at [25] (although his reasoning was not agreed with by the other Lords): 'It is now settled that legislation, primary or secondary, must be accorded an always-speaking construction unless the language and structure of the statute reveals an intention to impress on the statute a historic meaning. Exceptions to the general principle are a rarity'; *R (on the application of ZYN)* v. *Walsall Metropolitan BC* [2014] EWHC 1918 (Admin), [2015] 1 All ER 165 (Leggatt J adopting, in relation to interpreting 'Court of Protection', what he termed an 'updating' rather than an 'historical'

debate, it is clear that a statute may apply to circumstances which could not possibly have been foreseen at the time the statute was passed. It will be helpful to refer to some examples. I give six of these of which the penultimate is the most important.

In *Barker* v. *Wilson*,[52] the question in 1980 was whether the police were entitled under section 9 of the Bankers' Book Evidence Act 1879 to inspect microfilm of the bank's records. It was held that they were so entitled because the words 'bankers' books' should be interpreted to include microfilm. This was so even though no one in 1879 could possibly have envisaged the invention of microfilm and even though we might say that it is at the outer realm of plausible meanings for the word 'books' to encompass microfilm.

In *Royal College of Nursing of the UK* v. *Department of Health and Social Security*,[53] the question was whether abortions carried out under a new technique were lawful under the Abortion Act 1967. That Act legalised 'termination [of a pregnancy] by a registered medical practitioner'. Under the new technique, the abortion did not involve surgery or an injection by a doctor but comprised a nurse pumping a fluid into the womb. The nurse did so under the supervision of a doctor who would be on call but might not be present. It was held in the House of Lords, by a three to two majority, that such an abortion was covered by those words and was

interpretation). Cf. Lord Bingham in *R* v. *G* [2003] UKHL 50, [2004] 1 AC 1034, at [29] saying, with respect misleadingly, that the meaning of the expression itself cannot change.

[52] [1980] 1 WLR 884.   [53] [1981] AC 800.

therefore lawful. This was so even though in 1967 Parliament could not have envisaged the development of that mode of abortion. Lord Wilberforce was one of the dissentients but a passage from his judgment has subsequently been approved. His Lordship said:

> In interpreting an Act of Parliament it is proper, and indeed necessary, to have regard to the state of affairs existing, and known by Parliament to be existing, at the time. It is a fair presumption that Parliament's policy or intention is directed to that state of affairs ... [W]hen a new state of affairs, or a fresh set of facts bearing on policy, comes into existence, the courts have to consider whether they fall within the Parliamentary intention. They may be held to do so, if they fall within the same genus of facts as those to which the expressed policy has been formulated.[54] They may also be held to do so if there can be detected a clear purpose in the legislation which can only be fulfilled if the extension is made.[55]

[54] Similar to Lord Wilberforce's emphasis on the same 'genus' of facts was Lord Hoffmann's analysis in *Birmingham CC* v. *Oakley* [2001] 1 AC 617, 631, where his Lordship distinguished between the concept laid down by Parliament remaining the same, albeit that its content might change over time, and changing the concept. The latter was not a matter for the judiciary. That is correct, but the decision in the case itself (Lords Steyn and Clyde dissenting) took a needlessly narrow interpretation of the statutory wording.

[55] [1981] AC 800 at 822. Lord Wilberforce went on to say, 'In any event there is one course which the courts cannot take, under the law of this country; they cannot fill gaps; they cannot by asking the question "What would Parliament have done in this current case – not being one in contemplation – if the facts had been before it?" attempt themselves to supply the answer, if the answer is not to be found in the terms of the Act

In *R* v. *Secretary of State for Health ex parte Quintavalle*,[56] the question at issue was the interpretation of the word 'embryo'. The creation of human embryos outside the body was regulated by the Human Fertilisation and Embryology Act 1990. At the time the Act was passed, the only known method of creating an embryo involved fertilisation and in the Act an embryo was defined as 'a live human embryo where fertilisation is complete'. Subsequent to the Act, scientists developed a new method of creating an embryo – cell nuclear replacement – which did not involve fertilisation. Nevertheless it was held by the House of Lords that an embryo created by this new method was regulated by the Act and the words 'where fertilisation is complete' were interpreted as laying down the time at which an embryo should be treated as an embryo rather than being integral to the definition of an embryo. Again the important point is that it did not matter that no one in 1990 envisaged that embryos could be created other than by fertilisation and even though interpreting the Act in that way involved weakening the natural meaning of the words 'where fertilisation is complete'.

All three of those cases involved technological or medical developments not foreseen at the time the Act was passed; but that words can be given a modern meaning, in the light of their context and the purpose of the Act, is also shown in cases

itself.' The hypothetical question might be regarded as a useful way of thinking about the issue provided the answer that is arrived at falls within a plausible meaning of the words in the Act. But, with respect, it seems needlessly restrictive, and circular, to say that the answer has 'to be found in the terms of the Act itself'.

[56] [2003] UKHL 13, [2003] 2 AC 687.

that reflect changes in scientific thinking or societal attitudes. For example, in *R v. Ireland*,[57] in 1998, the House of Lords decided that causing or inflicting 'actual bodily harm' in sections 18, 20 and 47 of the Offences Against the Person Act 1861 includes causing or inflicting 'psychiatric illness'. Lord Steyn said:[58]

> The proposition that the Victorian legislator when enacting ss 18, 20 and 47 of the 1861 Act, would not have had in mind psychiatric illness is no doubt correct. Psychiatry was in its infancy in 1861. But ... the 1861 Act is ... 'always speaking' ... the statute must be interpreted in the light of the best current scientific appreciation of the link between the body and psychiatric injury.

A somewhat similar decision, albeit subjected to significant academic criticism,[59] was *Yemshaw* v. *Hounslow London*

---

[57] [1998] AC 147.   [58] Ibid. at 158–159.

[59] See, e.g., Richard Ekins (2013) *Law Quarterly Review* 17. See also the implied criticism by Justice James Edelman, 'Uncommon Statutory Interpretation' (2012) 11 TJR 71 at 89–93. He hints that it would be especially surprising if this were the position in criminal law: 'On the approach of the House of Lords it might be possible for a court to hold that a person would rightly have been acquitted of a crime based on a construction of a criminal statute in 1977, but that the words of the same unamended statute could acquire a new meaning so that in 2012 the person could now be convicted of the offence in exactly the same circumstances.' But surely an excellent and relatively uncontroversial example of that is *R v. Ireland*. Note also that, in so far as there has already been a binding decision on the point, the rules of precedent apply (see below at p. 27). See also, consistent with Justice Edelman's approach, the decision of the High Court of Australia (including Justice Edelman) in *Aubrey* v. *R* [2017] HCA 18, esp. at [30]. I am most grateful for discussions and email exchanges with Justice Edelman on the 'always speaking' doctrine, which has significantly helped to sharpen my thinking.

BC.[60] Here the question was whether a local authority's statutory obligation under the Housing Act 1996 to provide accommodation for the victims of 'violence' included, in the context of domestic violence, the victims of conduct that was not physical violence. The Supreme Court held that it did because, in the light of the purpose of the Act, 'violence' in the context of domestic violence should be given its modern meaning which went beyond physical violence to include all forms of intimidating behaviour and abuse giving rise to the risk of harm. Psychological as well as physical harm was included.[61] In the words of Lady Hale, giving the leading judgment of the Supreme Court:[62]

> [I]t is not for government and official bodies to interpret the meaning of the words which Parliament has used. That role lies with the courts. And the courts recognise that, where Parliament uses a word such as 'violence', the factual circumstances to which it applies can develop and change over the years ... The essential question ... is whether an updated meaning is consistent with the statutory purpose ... In this case, the purpose is to ensure that a person is not obliged to remain living in a home where she, her children or other members of her household are at risk of harm.

---

[60] [2011] UKSC 3, [2011] 1 WLR 433.

[61] Lady Hale, ibid. at [24], thought that, by the time of the Housing Act 1996, the meaning of (domestic) violence had already moved on from physical violence. However, crucially, she went on, 'But if I am wrong about that, there is no doubt that it has moved on now.'

[62] [2011] UKSC 3, [2011] 1 WLR 433 at [25]–[27].

Although it has come under fire, this is, in my view, an accurate statement of the judicial function in interpreting legislation. Very importantly, Lady Hale was not saying that the judges can update legislation. That would be to cross the line from interpreting to legislating. Rather what her Ladyship said was that, in so far as this fulfils the purpose of the statute, the judges may apply the contemporary meaning of the statutory words. To use the expression of Lord Wilberforce in the *Royal College of Nursing* case, the 'genus' in question in *Yemshaw* was 'violence', which now includes not only physical violence but also non-physical domestic violence.

There is an important footnote point here. Although sometimes not appreciated, it is clear that the rules of precedent apply in essentially the same way to judicial decisions on statutory interpretation as they do to the common law.[63]

---

[63] This is supported by Rupert Cross, *Precedent in English Law* (4th edn, Oxford, 1991) 178–182; F.A.R. Bennion, *Statutory Interpretation* (5th edn, Butterworths, 2008) 167–178; John Burrows and Ross Carter, *Statute Law in New Zealand* (4th edn, LexisNexis, 1990) 190–196; Lord Reid in *Goodrich* v. *Paisner* [1957] AC 65, 88 and in *London Transport Executive* v. *Betts* [1959] AC 211, 232; and Lord Wilberforce in *Jones* v. *Secretary of State for Social Services* [1972] AC 944. That precedent should apply to statutory interpretation is made especially clear when we consider some areas of statutory interpretation where there is such a mass of case law that it is easy to forget and that their basis is statutory rather than common law; e.g., the law on the Fatal Accidents Act 1976 (I have elsewhere referred to this as 'statute-based common law': see 'The Relationship between Common Law and Statute in the Law of Obligations' (2012) 128 *Law Quarterly Review* 232, 240). To recognise that precedent applies to statutory interpretation is of course not the same as saying that words in one statute should be given the same meaning in a different statute. Note also that there has been disagreement in the

The 'always speaking' doctrine therefore applies subject to the normal rules of precedent so that in *Yemshaw* the Supreme Court had to take into account that it was overruling an earlier decision of the Court of Appeal[64] on the meaning of 'violence' in the Housing Act 1986.[65]

Finally, in *Owens* v. *Owens*,[66] a divorce case, the Court of Appeal decided that although the marriage had broken down irretrievably, a divorce should not be granted to the wife because she had failed to prove her husband's behaviour was such that she could not reasonably be expected to live with him. Therefore, none of the grounds for divorce in section 1 of the Matrimonial Causes Act 1973 (re-enacting ss. 1–2 of the Divorce Reform Act 1969) had been established. Sir James Munby P, in the Court of Appeal, explained that where, as here, the Act was 'always speaking', it was necessary to construe it 'taking into account changes in our understanding of the natural world, technological changes, changes in social standards and, of particular importance here, changes in social

---

courts as to whether words that have been judicially interpreted should be given the same meaning where a statute has been re-enacted: see *Ex p Campbell* (1969) LR 5 Ch 703, 706; *Barras* v. *Aberdeen Steam Trawling and Fishing Co Ltd* [1933] AC 402, 412; *Farrell* v. *Alexander* [1977] AC 59; *R* v. *Chard* [1984] AC 279.

[64] *Danesh* v. *Kensington and Chelsea Royal London BC* [2006] EWCA Civ 1404, [2007] 1 WLR 69.

[65] For another recent example, in *R* v. *Taylor* [2016] UKSC 5, [2016] 4 All ER 617, the Supreme Court was asked, but refused, to use the 1966 Practice Statement to overrule the interpretation of s. 12A of the Theft Act 1968 (aggravated vehicle-taking) given a few years earlier by the Supreme Court in *R* v. *Hughes* [2013] UKSC 56, [2013] 4 All ER 613.

[66] [2017] EWCA Civ 182, [2017] 4 WLR 74.

attitudes'.[67] He cited in support of this *R* v. *Ireland* and explained that in the family law context what is covered by, for example, a 'child's welfare' (originally used in section 1 of the Guardianship of Infants Act 1925 now section 1 of the Children Act 1989) was to be judged by the standards of 2017, not those of 1925. It followed that the objective test in this case ('cannot reasonably be expected to live with [him]') should be judged by the standards of 2017, not those of 1969. The relevant standards were not those 'of the man or woman on the Routemaster clutching their paper bus ticket ... in ... 1969 ... but the man or woman on the Boris Bus with their Oyster Card in 2017'.[68] Yet, even applying the standards of 2017, when a wife might be reasonably expected to be less tolerant than in 1969, she had failed to make out her case.

I should add that the 'always speaking' doctrine also means the courts should take into account changes in the law since the Act in question was passed. A good example of this is that section 32(1)(c) of the Limitation Act 1980, which, for example, postpones the limitation period for restitution claims based on mistake, must now be read, after *Kleinwort Benson* v. *Lincoln City Council*,[69] as including mistakes of law as well as mistakes of fact. This is so even though at the time the Act was passed, prior to *Kleinwort Benson*, the law did not (subject to rare exceptions) allow restitution for mistakes of law.[70]

---

[67] Ibid. at [38]. Sir James Munby also cited *Birmingham City Council* v. *Oakley* [2001] 1 AC 617, 631 per Lord Hoffmann (see above note 54).

[68] Ibid. at [40].   [69] [1999] 2 AC 349.

[70] The equivalent of s 32(1)(c) was passed earlier this century and was re-enacted in the Limitation Acts 1939 and 1980. A final twist is that restitution has become so commonplace in the context of the restitution

We can therefore see from the 'always speaking' doctrine that a fundamental problem with reference to the legislator's intention (or indeed the understanding of the reader at the time) is not merely that we cannot ascertain that intention at a practical level but rather that it is directed to the wrong question. It is the wrong question because the right question is what is the best interpretation *now* of the Act. This is because the judges are interpreting a legal rule laid down in the public interest, which is not the same as interpreting interpersonal communications in everyday life. The judges must look for the best interpretation now of the legal rule laid down by those words. In deciding that, they must apply the statutory words in the light of their context and purpose. They can take into account the legislative history

of overpaid tax that, in order to protect the Revenue, s. 32(1)(c) has been statutorily abolished in the tax context: Finance Act 2004 s. 320; Finance Act 207, s. 107. Although no mention was made of the 'always speaking' doctrine and, instead, there were several (with respect) unhelpful references to what Parliament 'cannot have intended' or 'must have intended', *Littlewoods Ltd* v. *HMRC* [2017] UKSC 70, [2017] 3 WLR 1401 may be regarded as an interesting variant of the 'always speaking' doctrine in the context of legal changes. It was precisely because the Supreme Court was taking into account common law legal developments since the Value Added Tax 1994 was passed (i.e. the recognition in *Sempra Metals Ltd* v. *IRC* [2007] UKHL 34, [2008] 1 AC 561, that compound interest may be awarded as restitution of an unjust enrichment) that the relevant words of s. 78 of the 1994 Act ('if and to the extent that they would not be liable to do so apart from this section') were not best interpreted as preserving a common law claim. To do so, in the light of the right to compound interest at common law, would render the payment of simple interest under s. 78 a dead letter. Applying a purposive interpretation, as of today, the words should therefore be read as only preserving other statutory, and not common law, rights to interest.

including, albeit with heavy restrictions, Hansard; and fit with other legal rules, including common law rules, may also be important. This task of deciding on the best interpretation of a statute with the benefit of hindsight falls to the judges, and it is, in this sense, somewhat analogous to their role in interpreting a common law precedent (although, as I shall shortly explain, the words of a statute impose important constraints on statutory interpretation that do not apply to common law precedents). A serious objection to any reference to legislative intention is that it is advocating an approach that favours the law's ossification by inappropriately freezing the law in the past. We would not accept such an approach for the common law and there is no good reason why we should regard it as acceptable when interpreting legislation.

If the objection is that up-to-date interpretation gives too much power to the unelected judiciary, we might ask why this is not an even more obvious objection to the common law, the lifeblood of which is judicial updating. Yet the common law is widely held up as a system to be treasured and revered. And the judges, even though unelected, have proved themselves ideally qualified, through legal expertise and experience, to apply and develop the common law. Whether their role is interpreting statutes or developing the common law, the judges are clearly not free, as a legislator would be, simply to impose anew their own preferred policies. On the contrary, the statutory interpretative exercise is precisely constrained by the words, context and purpose of the statute. In any event, in our system of Parliamentary sovereignty, there is an ultimate check on judicial power because Parliament is always free to pass new or amending legislation overriding what the courts have decided.

In my second lecture, one of the questions I address is when, if ever, reform of the common law is best left to the Legislature. I there suggest that it is helpful to think of a sliding scale from 'lawyer's law' to law involving controversial social policy choices; and that the courts being unelected should exercise greater restraint at the higher end of the scale. The same question has rarely been overtly addressed in respect of (ordinary) statutory interpretation.[71] One reason for this is, no doubt, that we are already in a context where a statute is in play so there is no question of weighing up the general merits of statutory reform as against common law development. But another reason, again, is that reference to effecting the intention of Parliament has tended to obscure the courts' true role. The directly analogous question (to whether the judges should leave common law reform to the Legislature) is whether, even operating within the constraints of the statute's words, context and purpose, the courts should lay down a particular interpretation of the statute or should leave the matter for the Legislature to deal with by an express statutory amendment. While particular caution should be exercised if the matter is at the 'controversial social policy' end of the scale, I would suggest the Supreme Court should rarely, in practice, refrain from applying what it considers to be the best statutory interpretation on the ground that it is better left for a statutory amendment. This is not least because in

---

[71] Contrast conforming interpretation and the question of whether the courts should make a declaration of incompatibility under ss. 3–4 of the Human Rights Act 1998: see especially *R (Nicklinson)* v. *Ministry of Justice* [2014] UKSC 38, [2015] AC 657 (on which see lecture 2 note 92).

our system of Parliamentary sovereignty if the Legislature does not like the judicial interpretation, it is always free to reverse it.

Before I move on to my final part, I should interject to say, in relation to statutory interpretation generally, how useful I have found the seminal work of Professors Henry Hart and Albert Sacks on purposivism,[72] which I first studied at Harvard in 1980, and the more recent theory of 'dynamic statutory interpretation' put forward by Professor William Eskridge of Yale Law School.[73] In sharp contrast to the position in the UK, in the USA there has been a massive volume of writing on statutory interpretation, including by the judiciary. I cannot in a few sentences do justice to that body of scholarship but, suffice it to say here that, even putting to one side the deeper jurisprudential work of, for example, the late Professor Ronald Dworkin, especially his theory of fidelity to law,[74] various schools of thought in the USA on statutory interpretation can be identified, although each embraces a wide range of opinion. These include intentionalism and, within that, 'imaginative reconstruction' as

---

[72] Henry Hart and Albert Sacks, *The Legal Process: Basic Problems in the Making and Application of Law* (1958)(eds. William N. Eskridge and Philip P. Frickey, West Academic, 1994) 1374–1380.

[73] 'Dynamic Statutory Interpretation' (1987) 135 *University of Pennsylvania Law Review* 1479. See also William N. Eskridge, *Dynamic Statutory Interpretation* (Harvard University Press, 1994). See also Stephen Gageler, 'Common Law Statutes and Judicial Legislation: Statutory Interpretation as a Common Law Process' (2011) 37 *Monash University Law Review* 1 at 2: 'The attribution of meaning by courts to the statutory text ... resembles the declaration and development by courts of the common law.
The common law and statute law as applied by courts are, to a significant degree, products of the same inherently dynamic legal process.'

[74] Set out in Ronald Dworkin, *Law's Empire* (Harvard University Press, 1986).

favoured by, for example, Professor Roscoe Pound[75] and Judge Learned Hand;[76] textualism favoured by, for example, Professor John Manning,[77] Judge Easterbrook[78] and the late Justice Scalia;[79] and pragmatism as advocated by Judge Richard Posner.[80] Within the US literature, it seems to me that Hart and Sacks' purposivism, combined with Eskridge's 'dynamic statutory interpretation' – the latter brings out the close, albeit distinct, relationship between statutory and common law interpretation – is an approach that best captures what English courts are doing, and should be doing, when they interpret a statute.

4 Comparing and Contrasting Statutory and Contractual/Common Law Interpretation

In this final part, I want to consider how similar, or different, statutory interpretation is to other types of legal interpretation.

[75] 'Spurious Interpretation' (1907) 7 *Columbia Law Review* 379, esp. 381.

[76] See, e.g., *Lehigh Valley Coal Co* v. *Yensavage* 218 F 547, 553 (2d Cir, 1914); *Guiseppi* v. *Walling* 144 F 2d 608, 624 (2d Cir, 1944). For the term 'imaginative reconstruction', see Richard Posner, 'Statutory Interpretation – in the Classroom and in the Courtroom' (1983) 50 *University of Chicago Law Review* 800, 817.

[77] E.g. 'Textualism and the Equity of the Statute' (2001) 101 *Columbia Law Review* 1; 'Textualism and Legislative Intent' (2005) 91 *Virginia Law Review* 419.

[78] 'The Role of Original Intent in Statutory Interpretation' (1988) 11 *Harvard Journal of Law and Public Policy* 61.

[79] Antonin Scalia, *A Matter of Interpretation* (Princeton University Press, 1997).

[80] E.g. 'Statutory Interpretation – in the Classroom and in the Courtroom' (1983) 50 *University of Chicago Law Review* 800; Richard Posner, *The Problems of Jurisprudence* (Harvard University Press, 1990) 73–74.

So first, wearing my private lawyer's hat, I shall look at contractual interpretation before moving, secondly, to interpretation of common law precedents.

Contractual Interpretation

At first sight, the parallels between modern contractual interpretation and statutory interpretation are striking. In contract, we can view leading cases such as *Investors Compensation Scheme Ltd* v. *West Bromwich Building Soc*[81] and *Rainy Sky SA* v. *Kookmin Bank*[82] as representing a move away from an old literal to a modern contextual and purposive approach, just as with statutory interpretation. Indeed, at first sight, we might reasonably conclude that the only significant difference between the two types of interpretation is that, while after *Pepper* v. *Hart* the legislative history can be taken into account, in contract as laid down in *Chartbrook* v. *Persimmon Homes Ltd*[83] the contractual history – in the form of previous negotiations – cannot. Even there we see that the arguments for and against inclusion of the history follow a similar pattern with the cost of investigation and the irrelevance of most of the material being the two main arguments put against inclusion, while the potential

---

[81] [1998] 1 WLR 896.

[82] [2011] UKSC 50, [2011] 1 WLR 2900. See more recently *Arnold* v. *Britton* [2015] UKSC 36, [2015] AC 1619, which might be said to have marked a subtle move to steer interpretation back towards the words used being the primary factor of importance as against the commercial purpose. But in *Wood* v. *Capita Insurance Services Ltd* [2017] UKSC 24, [2017] AC 1173 1095, the Supreme Court sought to make clear that *Arnold* v. *Britton* did not cast any doubt on the approach in *Rainy Sky*.

[83] [2009] UKHL 38, [2009] 1 AC 1101.

occasional helpful relevance of the history is the main argument for inclusion. In other words, while *Chartbrook* v. *Persimmon* has gone the other way from *Pepper* v. *Hart*, there is a powerful argument that they should be consistent with each other whether that consistency is for or against exclusion.

Certainly, there are statements by commentators[84] and judges suggesting that the points of similarity between statutory and contractual interpretation outweigh any differences. In *Att-Gen of Belize* v. *Belize Telecom Ltd*,[85] Lord Hoffmann, giving the judgment of the Privy Council, referred to the search for the objective meaning in context as applying to all instruments whether 'a contract, a statute or articles of association'. And in the High Court of Australia in *Byrnes* v. *Kendle*,[86] Heydon and Crennan JJ spoke of the two types of interpretation as 'matching'

---

[84] Daniel Greenberg, *Craies on Legislation* (11th edn, Sweet & Maxwell, 2017) p. 774, after examining the modern approach to statutory interpretation, goes on to say in relation to commercial documents that: 'In the context of the construction of many documents that are not legislation similar principles to those [on statutory interpretation] apply.'

[85] [2009] UKPC 10, [2009] 1 WLR 1988 at [16]. And writing extra-judicially Lord Hoffmann, 'Judges, Interpretation and Self-Government' in *Lord Sumption and the Limits of Law* (eds. Nick Barber, Richard Ekins and Richard Yowell, Hart, 2016) 67 at 68 has written that, as regards treaties, contracts and statutes, 'the general principle of interpretation is the same and one cannot draw lines between the methods of interpreting one category of instruments and another'. See also *Pirelli Cable Holding NV* v. *Inland Revenue Commissioners* [2006] UKHL 4, [2006] 1 WLR 400, which concerned the statutory interpretation of tax provisions, in which Lord Nicholls said, at [13], 'Article 10, like all documents, must be interpreted purposively'. See further Oliver Wendell Holmes, 'The Theory of Legal Interpretation' (1899) 12 *Harvard Law Review* 417, 419.

[86] [2011] HCA 26, (2011) 243 CLR 253, at [98].

each other: '[t]he approach taken to statutory construction is matched by that which is taken to contractual construction'.

In my view, this assimilation thesis goes too far. While there are certainly important similarities, close examination reveals that there are also very significant differences.[87] I want to refer to four of them.[88]

---

[87] It follows from this that, where the parties to a contract 'contract in' to a statute that would otherwise not apply, the interpretation of the incorporated provisions is governed by the rules of contractual (not statutory) interpretation. But, in practice, it is very unlikely that this would produce a clash of interpretations because the normal assumption would be that the contracting parties objectively intend that the interpretation that would apply to the statute if free-standing would also apply if it were to be incorporated into the contract. See, generally, the discussion in *NRAM plc* v. *McAdam* [2015] EWCA Civ 751, [2016] 3 All ER 665 (where the question was whether the parties had validly 'contracted in' to the Consumer Credit Act 1974, even though the amount of credit was higher than that which triggered the protections in the Act). See also *Enviroco Ltd* v. *Farstad Supply A/S* [2009] EWCA Civ 1399 at [53]–[54]; *BNY Corporate Trustee Services Ltd* v. *Eurosail-UK 2007-3BL Plc* [2011] EWCA Civ 227, [2011] 1 WLR 2524; Daniel Greenberg, *Craies on Legislation* (11th edn, Sweet & Maxwell, 2017) paras. 18.1.13.7.2. See also the incorporation of 'model rules' into a contract (e.g. the standard express incorporation into documentary credits of the ICC Uniform Customs and Practice for Documentary Credits). In the reverse situation – the implementation by legislation of a treaty (a contract between states) – as, e.g., the implementation of the Hague–Visby Rules by the Carriage of Goods by Sea Act 1971, the principles of statutory interpretation apply, albeit that there are presumptions that there should be no breach of the State's international obligations and that implementation is consistent with the treaty's meaning: see Article 31 of the Vienna Convention on the Law of Treaties; Greenberg, *Craies on Legislation* paras. 18.1.13.8–18.1.13.9 and 29.1.2–29.1.2.2

[88] Another difference is that there is no direct statutory equivalent of an implied term: see obiter dicta of Akenhead J in *Aspect Contracts*

First, the role of intention has a more significant under-pinning role in relation to contractual interpretation than statutory interpretation because intention is far more significant in contract than in relation to statutes. I have expressed the view that reference to Parliamentary intention is a misleading fiction or mask. In contrast, the whole basis of contract – how it is that parties can create legally binding obligations as between themselves – may be said to rest on their agreement and hence on their common intentions. While practicality dictates that it is the objective intentions that principally count, few would suggest that intention is not of central importance in contract. This explains why there are doctrines concerned with impaired intention[89] in contract, such as misrepresentation, duress and undue influence, which have no role to play in respect of statutes. A statute is not rendered void or voidable because of a vitiating factor that impairs the intention of a relevant person. Similarly, there is no doctrine of incapacity that undermines an Act of Parliament.

A second difference, closely linked to the first, is that, while there is some scope for correcting drafting mistakes in statutes, by rectifying construction or rectification, this is much narrower under the leading *Inco* case[90] than under contractual rectifying construction or rectification of

---

(*Asbestos*) *Ltd* v. *Higgins Construction Plc* [2013] EWHC 1322 (TCC) at [17] (decision overruled, without mentioning this point, by the CA and the SC: see [2015] UKSC 38, [2015] 1 WLR 2961).

[89] 'Impaired intent' is the phrase adopted by Birks in describing the reason for restitution in unjust enrichment because of mistake, duress or undue influence: see Peter Birks, *Unjust Enrichment* (2nd edn, Oxford, 2005) 42.

[90] [2000] 1 WLR 586. See above p. 8.

a contract for mistakes.[91] Why is that so? Because as stressed by the House of Lords in the *Inco* case, great care must be taken to ensure that, in rectifying a statute, the judges do not cross the constitutionally central line between judicial interpretation and judicial legislation.

A third difference is that, in contrast to statutory interpretation – and subject to the contract clearly providing for this – contractual interpretation has no direct equivalent to the 'always speaking' idea.[92] Indeed, in relation to contract, where circumstances have significantly changed and this is not provided for in the contract; the contract may be automatically terminated under the doctrine of frustration.[93]

---

[91] For the law on rectification of contracts, see Andrew Burrows, *A Restatement of the English Law of Contract* (Oxford, 2016) pp. 183–187. The same point can be made about rectifying wills for mistakes, i.e. the doctrine of rectification for mistakes in the context of wills is far wider (see for that doctrine, *Marley* v. *Rawlings* [2014] UKSC 2, [2015] AC 129) than in respect of rectifying errors in statutes.

[92] Admittedly, it is not easy to compare the majority of contracts, which are short-term, with statutes that normally last indefinitely. However, even in relation to long-term contracts – and leaving aside where the parties have provided for changes – there appears to be little to support a contractual 'always speaking' doctrine, which would allow the courts to apply the best interpretation today of the words used in the contract by the parties. See, e.g., *Excelsior Group Productions Ltd* v. *Yorkshire Television Ltd* [2009] EWHC 1751 (Comm); *Globe Motors Inc* v. *TRW Lucas Varity Electric Steering Ltd* [2016] EWCA Civ 396, [2017] 1 All ER (Comm) 601; Kim Lewison, *The Interpretation of Contracts* (6th edn, Sweet & Maxwell, 2015) para. 5.15.

[93] Similarly, where circumstances have significantly changed, even a contract expressed to last indefinitely can usually be terminated on reasonable notice: *Staffordshire Area Health Authority* v. *South Staffordshire Waterworks Co* [1978] 1 WLR 1387.

In contrast, there is plainly no doctrine of frustration of statutes.

The final and most important difference is the importance of the boundary line for the courts. In respect of both contractual and statutory interpretation, there is a line that the judges have drawn which they cannot cross. In that sense, there is a similarity. On closer inspection, however, we see that the line is fundamentally different and reflects the very different exercise that the judges are involved in. If they stray over the line between contractual interpretation and making a contract for the parties, they stray into protecting one of the parties from a bad bargain even though the parties' consent was full and free thereby undermining freedom of contract. That may be thought problematic and unfortunate. But crossing the line between statutory interpretation and legislating is of far greater significance. It is a high constitutional principle that that line should not be crossed. To do so undermines the separation of powers between the judiciary and the Legislature.

Interpretation of Common Law Precedents

This leads finally to the interpretation of common law precedents, which I can deal with more briefly. As against power-conferring rules, allowing the creation or alteration of rights by the choice of parties – such as by contract, but also, for example, by wills and trusts – statutes and common law precedents both comprise laws laid down in the public interest. Perhaps not surprisingly, therefore, their interpretation shares some common features that differ from the interpretation of contracts.

So, particularly significant, common law precedents are 'always speaking' as is the general position, as we have seen, with statutes. Indeed, it is particularly obvious and uncontroversial that common law precedents are always speaking because updating is how the common law is developed; i.e., the principle is refined and applied for new situations and changes in attitudes. Again, as with statutes, ascertaining the intentions of the law-maker – here the judge – is not the ultimate aim of the interpretation;[94] and, just as with statutory interpretation, so with the interpretation of common law precedents – the role of the judges as against the Legislature is of fundamental constitutional importance.

If these similarities suggest that we might put the interpretation of statutes and common law precedents on one side of a line from the interpretation of contracts and the like on the other, it is important to clarify that I am not seeking to deny that there are important differences between

---

[94] For an excellent illustration of this, see Lord Hoffmann's judgment in the *Deutsche Morgan Grenfell* v. *IRC* [2006] UKHL 49 at [14] looking back at *Kleinwort Benson* v. *Lincoln CC* [1999] 2 AC 349: 'It is . . . neither here nor there for me to say that, as one who (in the end) gave wholehearted concurrence to Lord Goff's speech, I never thought that it had the meaning attributed to it by the Court of Appeal. Once a judgment has been published, its interpretation belongs to posterity and its author and those who agreed with him at the time have no better claim to be able to declare its meaning than anyone else. But to my mind the context in which Lord Goff made the remarks which I have quoted demonstrates conclusively that he could not have meant what the Court of Appeal thought.'

the interpretation of statutes and the interpretation of common law precedents. Of course, there are. Statutory interpretation, even though purposive and contextual, and, in general, always speaking, is controlled ultimately by the words used – just as is contractual interpretation – in a way that the interpretation of common law precedents is not. Indeed, judges often say that we must not treat the words of a judgment as if they are a statute. Closely linked to this is that classic common law interpretation involves reasoning by analogy. We take the principle of the decision and apply it by analogy to new facts. That is different from interpreting statutes, although the long discredited idea of the 'equity of the statute' did appear to allow that.[95] As Dworkin expressed it in *Law's Empire*: 'judges and lawyers do not think that the force of precedents is exhausted, as a statute would be, by the linguistic limits of some particular phrase';[96] and, a few pages on, he wrote, 'the fairness of treating like cases alike ... [provides a] general explanation of the gravitational force of precedent [and] accounts for the feature that defeated the enactment theory, which is that the force of a precedent escapes the language of its opinion.'[97] Put another way, in interpreting a statute,

---

[95] For a recent illuminating rejection of it, see *Singularis Holdings Ltd* v. *Pricewaterhouse Coopers* [2014] UKPC 36, [2015] AC 1675, esp. at [78]–[83].

[96] Ronald Dworkin, *Law's Empire* (Harvard University Press, 1986) at 111.

[97] Ibid. at 113. See also 'statutory interpretation ... depends upon the availability of a canonical form of words ... that set limits to the ... decisions that the statute may be taken to have made' (p. 110); 'the earlier decision exerts a gravitational force on later decisions even when these later decisions lie outside its particular orbit' (p. 111); 'The gravitational force of precedent cannot be captured by any theory that takes the full force of precedent to be its enactment force as a piece of legislation' (p. 112).

unlike a common law precedent, the judges are constrained by the plausible meanings of the statute's words. So a statute applying to dogs cannot be applied to cats; a statute applying to pneumoconiosis cannot be applied to asbestosis; and a statute applying to motor vehicles cannot be applied to pedal bicycles. This is so even if the purpose behind the statute might be regarded as equally applicable to the other categories. Although there are exceptions where the statute is drafted at a high level of principle, or otherwise invites analogous reasoning, the words of a statute, even though always speaking, typically do not allow analogous reasoning whereas reasoning by analogy – principled reasoning to ensure that like cases are treated alike – is the lifeblood of the common law. Statutes, like contracts, carry a limiting linguistic force that does not apply in the same way to common law precedents.

Conclusion

There are three 'take-home' messages from this lecture.

(i) Legal academics and law students in this jurisdiction should be devoting far more time to thinking coherently and at a practical level about the law on statutory interpretation.

(ii) The justified modern approach in this jurisdiction to statutory interpretation is that it is concerned to determine the best meaning today of the statutory words, in the light of their context and purpose; but that, contrary to the judicial tradition, all reference to Parliamentary intention is best avoided. While it is constitutionally imperative that the courts respect the line between interpreting and legislating, rational transparency renders it unacceptable for the courts' true reasoning to be hidden by the fiction or mask of 'Parliamentary intention'.

(iii) Although at first sight attractive, the idea that we can assimilate the interpretation of statutes with contracts goes too far; and, again, although both are concerned with the interpretation of laws laid down in the public interest, the interpretation of statutes also differs significantly from the interpretation of common law precedents. To use a rather clichéd idiom, those three types of interpretation may not be apples, oranges and bananas but they are, at least, different types of apple.

Lecture 2

The Interaction between Common Law and Statute

As Professor Guido Calabresi said in his book, *A Common Law for the Age of Statutes*,[1] we are 'choking on statutes'.[2] In Grant Gilmore's graphic description, for the past century and more, there has been 'an orgy of statute-making'.[3] And in the words of Professor Robert Stevens, 'Judge-made rules are ... doomed to die ... Eventually legislation will cover all, as far as the eye can see.'[4]

Of course, in common law systems, our basic law is judge-made. Statutes are seen as supplementing or removing the common law but it is the common law that provides the residual gapless law where there is no statute. So whatever the factual takeover of the common law by statute, and hence the factual dominance of statutes, in a conceptual sense, our common law remains the primary source of law. This contrasts with civilian systems where a statutory code is seen as providing the basic gapless law.[5]

---

[1] Guido Calabresi, *A Common Law for the Age of Statutes* (Harvard University Press, 1982).
[2] Ibid. at 1. [3] *The Ages of American Law* (1977) at 95.
[4] 'Private Law and Statute' at 1 (paper given at conference on Private Law in the 21st Century, Brisbane, 2015).
[5] For a fascinating insight into the creation of the French Code Civil, see the editorial notes of Professor Thomas Barnes to the Legal Classics version

However, the relative neglect of the study of statutes in a common law system is only partly to be attributed to the conceptual centrality of the common law. It is also because, at least on the face of it, cases are so much more interesting and entertaining than statutes. As lawyers in the common law tradition, we are never happier than when we have cases to learn from. Case law is fun because we have a real-life situation at the forefront of attention. Thinking just about contract and tort, we have skiing holidays that do not live up to expectations, swimming pools that are not built to the correct depth, tragedies at bluebell time in Kent, nephews who ignore

of the Code Civil (kindly lent to me by Sir Stephen Sedley). This makes clear how influential Napoleon Bonaparte was on the drafting of that code. A first draft was produced in a few months by four jurists working 'under the relentless pressure' (p. 8) of Napoleon. There followed three years of painstaking reworking of the draft by the eminent jurists who made up the Conseil D'Etat. Their deliberations involved 123 sittings and Napoleon presided at 55 of them. Although not a lawyer, Barnes writes that 'His interventions at the *Conseil* were many, spontaneous, usually sensible and always practical, aimed at ensuring simplicity in wording and – surprisingly perhaps for one conventionally accounted an autocrat – generally directed toward greater liberality' (p. 8). The drafters knew that their first and demanding reader would be Napoleon himself. He 'was a close reader for he had definite ideas of what legal reform should do and what the law should be' (p. 9). During these years (1800–1804) Napoleon was not fighting battles and was seeking domestic greatness through his reforms of French institutions. In exile he is reported as having said (Frederich CJ,'The Ideological and Philosophical Background' in *The Code Napoleon and the Common Law World* (ed. Bernard Schwartz, New York University Press, 1956) p. 17 n. 20): 'My glory is not to have won forty battles, for the defeat at Waterloo will erase the memory of as many victories. What nothing will destroy, what will live eternally, is my *Code Civil* . . . '

the agreements made with their now deceased uncles, and balls being hit into gardens from the village cricket field. The range of human life in the law reports is boundless. With statutes, in contrast, we have abstract rules with no real-life facts to help and this makes their study and understanding dry and difficult.

Part of my aim in these lectures is to bring alive, at a practical level, the study of statutes. Lecture 1 has examined the interpretation of statutes while Lecture 3 looks at the improvement of statute law. But in a common law system, there are particularly intriguing questions about the interaction between common law and statute – and that interaction (the second 'i' of the three) is the theme of this lecture.[6] I have divided what I want to say into three parts:[7] first, developing the common law by analogy to statutes; secondly, removing the common law, or freezing its development, by statute; and, thirdly, as regards reforming the common law, should it be by judicial development or by statute?

---

[6] In the context of tort and statutes, see generally on this interaction T.T. Arvind and Jenny Steele, 'Introduction: Legislation and the Shape of Tort Law' in *Tort Law and the Legislature* (eds. T.T. Arvind and Jenny Steele, Hart, 2013) ch. 1.

[7] There are, of course, other questions on the interaction between common law and statute that I do not discuss; and my choice of topics may reflect my interests as a private rather than a public lawyer (although I do discuss the 'principle of legality' within part 2 in the context of the removal of the common law). Certainly, from a public law perspective, the very basis of judicial review may be thought to rest on one's view as to the interaction between common law and statute: for an enlightening discussion, see, e.g., Paul Craig, *UK, EU and Global Administrative Law: Foundations and Challenges*, Hamlyn Lectures 2014 (Cambridge, 2015) 125–155.

1 Developing the Common Law by Analogy to Statutes

The common law is a system built on analogical development. New precedents are laid down by the judges treating the new facts of the instant case as analogous to those covered by existing precedent. However, the question I am here asking is: can we develop the common law not merely by analogy to the existing common law but also by analogy to statutes?[8]

The argument in principle for allowing the analogical use of statutes in developing the common law – or as it has sometimes been phrased allowing statutes to have 'gravitational force'[9] –is a powerful one. Not only are statutes a valuable resource for enriching the common law but coherence across the whole of the laws of a legal system, so that like cases are treated alike, should be an important goal. Professor Jack Beatson, now Lord Justice Beatson, attacked what he termed the 'oil and water' approach to the relationship between common law and statute, which sees them as separate non-intermingling sources of law such that there can be no use of

---

[8] For a general examination of reasoning by analogy in the common law, see Grant Lamond, 'Analogical Reasoning in the Common Law' (2014) 34 *Oxford Journal of Legal Studies* 567. At 568, Lamond expressly excludes using statutes as a source of analogy from his examination because, inter alia, 'their use is more limited and complex than the use of cases'.

[9] See, e.g., Peter Cane, 'Taking Disagreement Seriously: Courts, Legislatures and the Reform of Tort Law' (2005) 25 *Oxford Journal of Legal Studies* 393 at 399. The term 'gravitational force' was originally used by Dworkin (see, e.g., Ronald Dworkin, *Law's Empire* (Harvard University Press, 1986) 111–112) to explain the force of a common law precedent.

statutes by analogy.[10] As he rhetorically put it: 'Why should statutory manifestations of principle ... not be part of the armoury of the common law judge in determining a hard case and seeking to determine what best fits the fundamental principles of the legal system?'[11]

In a seminal article in the *Harvard Law Review* in 1908,[12] Professor Roscoe Pound set out a four-fold categorisation of the possible impact of statute on the common law. His categories 3 and 4 involved no use of statute by analogy in developing the common law. Category 2 saw statute being used by analogy in developing the common law but having the same status as common law precedents, whereas category 1 saw statute as not only being used by analogy in developing the common law but as an analogy of superior status to common law precedents. According to Pound, it was inevitable that over time there would be a progression from category 4 to category 1. In his words, '[I]t is submitted that the course of legal development upon which we have entered already must lead us to adopt the method of the second and eventually the method of the first.'[13]

Writing in 1961, Sir Rupert Cross suggested that English law fell within category 2[14] (i.e. a statute could be used by analogy in developing the common law but it had no

---

[10] Jack Beatson, 'The Role of Statute in the Development of Common Law Doctrine' (2001) 117 *Law Quarterly Review* 247.

[11] Ibid. at 252.

[12] 'Common Law and Legislation' (1908) 21 *Harvard Law Review* 383.

[13] Ibid. at 385.

[14] *Precedent in English Law* (1st edn, Clarendon, 1961) 166–169. See also Sir Rupert Cross and Jim Harris (4th edn, Clarendon, 1991) 173–176.

greater status than a common law precedent). Yet this has been regarded as a controversial description of the approach in English law. Beatson implied that Cross' analysis was overoptimistic and Professor Patrick Atiyah in a well-known article, 'Common Law and Statute Law',[15] in the *Modern Law Review* in 1985 expressly disagreed with Cross and argued, in effect, that English law fell within category 3 or 4 and had not moved to category 2 so that the courts did not generally accept the use of statutes by analogy in developing the common law. With great respect to Atiyah, Cross was plainly correct.[16] On close inspection, there are many examples in English law of the courts developing the common law by analogy to statute. And although it may be true to say that the range of examples has widened since Atiyah's article was written, some of the examples I am about to give are very long-standing. So here are eight examples of statutes being used by analogy in the development of the common law.[17]

---

[15] (1985) 48 *Modern Law Review* 1.

[16] Atiyah's argument against that being the correct analysis rests, with respect, on incorrectly treating the non-use by the courts of a statutory analogy because that analogy would be inappropriate – for example, where it would undermine a statute or would contradict the desired direction of the common law – as if it were rejecting analogous reasoning as impermissible.

[17] Two further examples are as follows: (i) In *Erven Warnik BV v. J Townend & Sons (Hull) Ltd* [1979] AC 731, the policy of several statutes was used by the House of Lords to decide that a wider, rather than a narrower, scope should be given to the tort of passing off; (ii) In *Re D'Jan of London Ltd* [1993] BCC 646 at 648, in deciding on the standard of the duty of care owed to a company by a director at common law, the court drew on s. 214 of the Insolvency Act 1986 which deals with the duty of care of a director in the context of wrongful trading where a company has become insolvent.

(i) The long-established general common law presumption, that a person is presumed dead where absent or unheard of for seven years, was an analogy drawn from earlier statutes relating to bigamy and the continuation of lives on which leases were held.[18]

(ii) Statutory limitation periods, such as the general six-year limitation period for a claim for damages in tort, have long been applied by analogy to claims for equitable relief (such as equitable compensation or an account of profits for breach of fiduciary duty); and that is expressly recognised in section 36(1) of the Limitation Act 1980.[19]

(iii) The implied terms under the then Sale of Goods Act 1893[20] were applied, by analogy, to contracts for work and materials before statute (the Supply of Goods and Services Act 1982) later intervened to imply those terms into such contracts.[21]

---

[18] *Doe* v. *Nepean* (1833) 5 B & Ad 86 at 94.

[19] For discussion, see, e.g., *Gwembe Valley Development Co Ltd* v. *Koshy* [2003] EWCA Civ 1048, [2004] 1 BCLC 131; *P & O Nedlloyd BV* v. *Arab Metals Co, The UB Tiger* [2006] EWCA Civ 1717, [2007] 1 WLR 2288. Section 36(1) is one of the most opaque provisions in our statute book requiring, as it does, delving back into pre-1940 history. The subsection reads that various limitation periods under the 1980 Act 'shall not apply in any claim for specific performance of a contract or for any injunction or for other equitable relief, except in so far as any such time limit may be applied by the court by analogy in like manner as the corresponding time limit under any enactment repealed by the Limitation Act 1939 was applied before 1st July 1940'.

[20] Now the Sale of Goods Act 1979.   [21] *Samuels* v. *Davis* [1943] KB 526.

(iv) In the famous case of *Parry* v. *Cleaver*,[22] in deciding that a disability pension should not be deducted in assessing damages for personal injury, the House of Lords drew on the analogy of section 2(1) of the Fatal Accidents Act 1959, which laid down that pensions should not be deducted in assessing damages for wrongful death.

(v) In *Universe Tankships Inc of Monravia* v. *International Transport Workers' Federation, The Universe Sentinel*,[23] the statutory trade dispute defence to torts was held to be applicable by analogy (albeit not made out on the facts) to a claim for restitution of money paid under duress. In other words, in working out what constituted illegitimate economic duress in the common law of unjust enrichment, the House of Lords relied on where statute had drawn the line between acceptable and unacceptable trade union behaviour for the purposes of the economic torts.

(vi) In determining the standard of the duty of care of a financial adviser, the courts have drawn on statutory financial regulatory rules.[24]

(vii) The recognition in, for example, *Mahmud* v. *Bank of Credit and Commerce Int SA*[25] of the implied term not to destroy mutual trust and confidence in a contract of

---

[22] [1970] AC 1. [23] [1983] 1 AC 366.

[24] See, e.g., *Seymour* v. *Ockwell* [2005] EWHC 1137 (QB), [2005] PNLR 39, at [77]; *Shore* v. *Sedgwick Financial Services Ltd* [2007] EWHC 2059 (QB), [2008] PNLR 10, at [161] (upheld on a separate point at [2008] EWCA Civ 863, [2008] PNLR 37). I am grateful to Professor Gerard McMeel for this example.

[25] [1998] AC 20.

employment was inspired by the statutory law on unfair dismissal. As Professor Mark Freedland has expressed it, '[That implied term] was a contractual conception which evolved from and was shaped by the technical demands and policy considerations of the statute law of unfair dismissal.'[26] In the context of employment law, there is also Lord Hoffmann's well-known statement in *Johnson* v. *Unisys Ltd*[27] when he said: 'Judges in developing the law must have regard to the policies expressed by Parliament in legislation ... [The judges'] traditional function is to adapt and modernise the common law. But such developments must be consistent with legislative policy as expressed in statutes. The courts may proceed in harmony with Parliament but there should be no discord.' However, it is important to recognise that, while at first sight this might be thought to offer strong support for developing the common law by analogy to statutes, the statement was actually made in the context of holding back, rather than developing, the common law and the decision in the case, as I shall explain shortly, is highly controversial for that reason.

(viii) The modern development of the tort of privacy from the equitable wrong of breach of confidence has drawn

---

[26] Mark Freedland, *The Personal Employment Contract* (2003) at 303. See also Anne Davies, 'The Relationship between the Contract of Employment and Statute' in *The Contract of Employment* (general editor, Mark Freedland, Oxford, 2016) 73, 83.

[27] [2001] UKHL 13, [2003] 1 AC 518 at [37].

on the ECHR right to respect for family and private life, given effect in the UK by the Human Rights Act 1998.[28]

In the light of these examples – added to the fundamental argument that coherence dictates that, as far as possible, like cases should be treated alike across common law and statute – it should be clearly accepted that the English courts do not, and should not, regard reasoning by analogy from statutes to develop the common law as in any sense illegitimate. Although he was speaking of New Zealand law, Sir Robin Cooke expressed the point succinctly and clearly in *South Pacific Manufacturing Co Ltd* v. *NZ Security Consultants and Investigations Ltd*, where he said:[29] 'the analogy of a statute may properly influence the development of the common law'.

---

[28] See, e.g., *Campbell Mirror Group Newspapers Ltd* [2004] UKHL 22, [2004] 2 AC 457.

[29] [1992] 2 NZLR 282, 298. An excellent example of this in New Zealand is provided by *National Bank of New Zealand Ltd* v. *Waitaki International Processing (NI) Ltd* [1999] 2 NZLR 211 in which the 'contributory negligence' approach, adopted as an interpretation of the statutory change of position defence laid down in s. 94 of the Judicature Act 1908, has been applied by analogy to the common law defence of change of position. For the view that it is more complex to apply a statute by analogy in Australia, because it is a federal jurisdiction so that there may not be a consistent pattern of legislation, see *Esso Australia Resources Ltd* v. *Commissioner of Taxation of Commonwealth of Australia* (1999) 201 CLR 49, 61: England was specifically contrasted as having a 'single Parliament' and as being a 'unitary system'. But for the view that Australian (private) common law would benefit from an increased emphasis on coherence with statute, see Elise Bant, 'Statute and Common Law: Interaction and Influence in Light of the Principle of Coherence' (2015) 38 *University of New South Wales Law Journal* 367.

Take further a hypothetical illustration. Say the Supreme Court was required to decide on the retention of the traditional restriction, that a failure of consideration must be total before there can be restitution of money paid under a void contract or a contract that has been terminated for breach. In addition to some cases, which may be said to cast doubt on that total failure requirement,[30] it would surely be a valid argument that the Law Reform (Frustrated Contracts) Act 1943 reformed the law on restitution after termination of a contract for frustration by departing from any requirement that the failure of consideration be total. That statute could surely be used by analogy in developing the common law outside the context of frustration.[31]

This illustration also assists in clarifying that Cross was correct in positioning English law in the second of Pound's categories rather than the first. English courts would, it is submitted, feel comfortable in using the Law Reform (Frustrated

---

[30] E.g. *Rowland* v. *Divall* [1923] 2 KB 500. See generally Andrew Burrows, *The Law of Restitution* (3rd edn, Oxford, 2011) 324–326.

[31] Similarly, if the Supreme Court were to be asked to decide whether to extend the pre-contractual duty of disclosure from its present relatively narrow limits at common law (see *Banque Financiere de la Cite SA* v. *Westgate Insurance Co Ltd* [1991] 2 AC 249), it would surely be appropriate for the courts to take into account statutory pre-contractual duties of disclosure such as those to be found in the Consumer Credit Act 1974, rr 7–8 of the Package Travel, Package Holiday and Package Tours Regulations 1992 (SI 1992/3288), the Financial Services and Markets Act 2000, and the Consumer Contracts (Information, Cancellation and Additional Charges) Regulations 2013 (SI 2013/3134). Beatson makes this argument in *Has the Common Law a Future* (1996) at 24–31. See also Sir Jack Beatson, Andrew Burrows and John Cartwright, *Anson's Law of Contract* (30th edn, Oxford, 2016) 372–373.

Contracts) Act 1943 alongside the common law 'exceptions' to the requirement of total failure of consideration. But they would not consider that that statutory analogy was superior to the common law analogies. After all this is a development of the common law and there is no question of the statute directly applying as a matter of straightforward statutory interpretation. English law therefore fits within the second category where a statutory analogy can be relied on in developing the common law but is not necessarily regarded as superior to standard common law reasoning by analogy.

It is important to add, by way of clarification, that I am not suggesting that all statutes lend themselves to being used by analogy in developing the common law. Some statutes further a very specific and narrow policy that it would be inappropriate to apply by analogy to the common law. Nor am I suggesting that, just because there is a statutory analogy which could be used in developing the common law, that statutory analogy must be so applied. It is a matter for the courts to decide whether it is appropriate to use a statute by analogy in developing the common law. The important point to accept is that there should be no bar to such a use of statutes. Reasoning by analogy from a statute to develop the common law should not be regarded as illegitimate.

2 Removing the Common Law, or Freezing Its Development, by Statute

I now turn to the second part of this lecture, which takes us in the opposite direction from the first. Whereas the first part looked at developing the common law by the use of statute, we are here turning to the removal of the common law, or freezing its development, by statute. Within this part, I am asking three questions. First, has statute removed an area of the common law or, on the contrary, does the common law co-exist with the statute? Secondly, assuming the common law co-exists with the statute, has its development nevertheless been frozen by statute? And, thirdly, a question that has so excited constitutional lawyers: what is the impact on the removal of the common law of applying the 'principle of legality' in interpreting a statute?

Before I move to those three questions, there is a preliminary point that may seem obvious but is often overlooked. This is that almost every statute that we can think of depends to a greater or lesser extent on the survival or preservation of *some* of the common law. In other words, in the common law tradition, very few, if any, statutes are completely self-contained. Nothing that I here say is intended to deny that clearly correct observation. As Atiyah elegantly put it, '[A] new statute becomes part of a very large body of law even though not one word is said about these things in the Act itself.'[32] Take, for example, the Contracts (Rights of Third Parties) Act 1999. In certain circumstances, most obviously where the contracting parties have expressly provided for this, the statute allows a third party to enforce a contract. So by section 1(1), '[A] person who is not a party to a contract (a "third party") may in his own right enforce a term of the

---

[32] P.S. Atiyah 'Common Law and Statute Law' (1985) 48 *Modern Law Review* 1, 2.

contract if (a) the contract expressly provides that he may.' Plainly, this statute depends on the survival of the common law of contract in the sense that the institution of binding contracts must exist for this statute to apply and, as there is no interpretation section in the 1999 Act, we have to turn to the common law to know what is meant by a contract, a term of a contract and a party to the contract. No doubt those drafting statutes are all too well aware of the necessity of 'reading into' a statute the background common law. It would make the task of drafting almost impossible if no assumptions as to that background could be made. This basic point also explains straightaway why we cannot regard common law and statute as unmixed independent bodies of law – 'oil and water' in the traditional metaphor – and why it is a mistake to try to understand most statutes without first being versed in the common law.

Has Statute Removed the Common Law or Does the Common Law Co-Exist with the Statute?

Sometimes the statute expressly deals with this question. An example of this is the Occupiers' Liability Act 1957.[33] Section 1(1) states:

---

[33] The identical wording 'in place of the rules of the common law' is also used in s. 1(1) of the Occupiers' Liability Act 1984, which lays down the duty of an occupier to those who are not his lawful visitors, most obviously trespassers. Similarly, s. 1(1) of the Animals Act 1971 expressly sets out the areas of the common law that are being replaced:
'The provisions of sections 2 to 5 of the Act replace – (a) the rules of the common law imposing a strict liability in tort for damage done by an

The rules enacted by the two next following sections shall
have effect, in place of the rules of the common law, to
regulate the duty which an occupier of premises owes to his
visitors in respect of dangers due to the state of the
premises or to things done or omitted to be done on
them.[34]

The common law of unjust enrichment has also plainly been
excluded by section 80(7) of the Value Added Tax Act 1994
dealing with overpaid VAT. The relevant wording is as
follows:

Except as provided by this section, the Commissioners
shall not be liable to credit or repay any amount accounted
for or paid to them by way of VAT that was not VAT due to
them.[35]

Even if, as is usually the case, there is no express
reference to the replacement of the common law, or to the
statute being an exclusive regime, it will often be clear that the
statute does replace the common law and what the essential
scope of that replacement is. So, for example, the Contracts
(Rights of Third Parties) Act 1999 does not expressly say that it
is amending the common law doctrine of privity of contract.

---

animal on the ground that the animal is regarded as ferae naturae or that
its vicious and mischievous propensities are known or presumed to be
known . . . (c) the rules of the common law imposing a liability for cattle
trespass.'

[34] The ambit of these words was considered in *Ferguson* v. *Welsh* [1987] 1
WLR 1553.

[35] See for the same essential wording, the Customs and Excise Management
Act 1979, s. 137A(5).

However, it is clear that, to avoid undermining the Act, where the provisions apply, the common law privity restriction has been removed.[36] Plainly, it would be no answer to a claim brought by a third party under the Act for the defendant to argue that such a claim would infringe classic common law precedents insisting on privity and denying third party rights, such as *Tweddle* v. *Atkinson*,[37] *Dunlop Pneumatic Tyre Co Ltd* v. *Selfridge*,[38] and *Beswick* v. *Beswick*.[39] To allow such an argument would make a nonsense of the Act.

Those are easy examples. In relation to some other statutes, it is a difficult question of statutory interpretation whether a statute should be seen as an exclusive regime, replacing the common law, or as a regime sitting alongside the common law and providing an alternative source of rights for claimants. Two decisions of the House of Lords in the last 15 years may serve as helpful illustrations.[40]

---

[36] In contrast, by not mentioning the privity doctrine, it is also implicit that, where the provisions of the Act do not apply, the common law privity doctrine does survive to deny a claim by a third party. Again, there are provisions which expressly mark out the extent of the reform. It might have been thought, e.g., that the regime of third party rights under the Act was intended to be an exclusive regime so that it supplanted existing exceptions to the privity doctrine at common law (such as the trust of the promise). That is not so. Section 7(1) clarifies, by enacting that section 1 of the Act 'does not affect any right or remedy of a third party that exists or is available apart from the Act', that that was not the purpose. In other words, the wide-ranging exception to privity created by the Act sits alongside, rather than replacing, other exceptions to privity.

[37] (1861) 1 B & S 393.   [38] [1915] AC 847.   [39] [1968] AC 58.

[40] For another recent example, see *PST Energy 7 Shipping LLC* v. *OW Bunker Malta Ltd, The Res Cogitans* [2016] UKSC 23, [2016] AC 1034, on the question whether s. 49 Sale of Goods Act 1989 is an exclusive code

In *Marcic* v. *Thames Water Utilities Ltd*,[41] a householder had had to suffer the unpleasant experience of the sewers periodically flooding into his home and garden. One of the questions was whether he could bring a claim against the public water authority in the tort of nuisance or whether the statutory scheme under the Water Industry Act 1991 was an exclusive regime so that the appropriate redress was to be sought through the regulator of the water industry – the Director General of Water Services – who should first issue enforcement orders. The House of Lords unanimously decided

---

governing when a seller is entitled to the remedy of the award of the price. See also *R (Child Poverty Action Group)* v. *Secretary of State for Work and Pensions* [2010] UKSC 54, [2011] 2 AC 15 (discussed below at 73). For other excellent illustrations, see on the question whether s. 33 and Sch 1AB of the Taxes Management Act 1970, dealing with the overpayment of income tax and capital gains tax, is exclusive of the common law of unjust enrichment: *Woolwich Equitable Building Soc* v. *IRC* [1993] AC 70, esp. at 176; *Deutsche Morgan Grenfell Group Plc* v. *IRC* [2006] UKHL 49, [2007] 1 AC 558; *Monro* v. *HMRC* [2008] EWCA Civ 306, [2009] Ch 69. In *Littlewoods Ltd* v. *HMRC* [2017] UKSC 70, it was decided that s. 78(1) of the Value Added Tax Act 1994, which allows simple interest only to be awarded where restitution of overpaid sums of VAT is being made by HMRC under s. 80 of the 1994 Act, is exclusive of the common law which now allows compound interest applying *Sempra Metals Ltd* v. *IRC* [2007] UKHL 34, [2008] 1 AC 561.

[41] [2003] UKHL 66, [2004] 2 AC 42. See also *Dobson* v. *Thames Water Utilities* [2007] EWHC 2021 (TCC), [2008] 2 All ER 362; reversed in part [2009] EWCA Civ 28, [2009] 3 All ER 319. For a detailed examination of the *Marcic* case, in the context of the 'pre-emption' of the common law by statute, see Maria Lee, 'Occupying the Field: Tort and the Pre-Emptive Statute' in *Tort Law and the Legislature* (eds. T.T. Arvind and Jenny Steele, Hart, 2013) ch. 18.

that to allow a claim in the tort of nuisance would be inconsistent with the statutory scheme for redress under the 1991 Act. Although section 18(8) of the Act expressly preserved remedies for *available* common law causes of action, their Lordships held that a common law cause of action in nuisance would clash with the statute and was therefore not available. The statutory scheme was an exclusive regime. In Lord Nicholls' words:

> The existence of a parallel common law right, whereby individual householders who suffer sewer flooding may themselves bring court proceedings when no enforcement order has been made, would set at nought the statutory scheme. It would effectively supplant the regulatory role the director was intended to discharge when questions of sewer flooding arise.[42]

In contrast, going the other way, is *Revenue and Customs Commissioners* v. *Total Network SL*.[43] Here the House of Lords, by a three-two majority, decided that HMRC could succeed in their claim for damages for the tort of unlawful means conspiracy in respect of a VAT fraud, despite their statutory powers to recover VAT under the Value Added Tax Act 1994. The minority (Lords Hope and Neuberger) reasoned that the tort claim was a means of collecting VAT not provided for in the 1994 Act, which was a comprehensive and exclusive code. They argued that it would be inconsistent to allow claims both under the Act and at common law. But the majority (Lords Scott, Walker and Mance) saw no such inconsistency and equated

---

[42] Ibid. at [35].   [43] [2008] UKHL 19, [2008] 1 AC 1174.

the claim to one where tax was stolen from the Commissioners. Lord Walker said:

> The commissioners do not now handle large sums of cash, since there are safer means for the transfer of money. But if an official vehicle carrying cash belonging to the commissioners (cash representing collected taxes) were hijacked and the cash stolen, it seems to me that the commissioners would undoubtedly have a civil remedy available to reclaim it, if the robbers were apprehended and the proceeds of the robbery traced to a bank account. In my opinion, the present case is essentially the same.[44]

What those cases and others like them show is that whether an area of the common law has by implication been removed by a statute is often a difficult question of statutory interpretation; and commonly this will turn on the courts' perception of whether the common law and statutory regimes are inconsistent or, on the contrary, can happily co-exist.

Has the Statute Frozen the Development of the Common Law?

Within this second part of my lecture, I now move to my second question (which is very closely linked to the first). Assuming that a particular area of the common law survives, does the statute nevertheless freeze ordinary common law development? Professor Anne Davies has called this

---

[44] Ibid. at [109]. In the words of Lord Mance, at [130], '[I]t seems to me that the statute must be positively shown to be inconsistent with the continuation of the ordinary common law remedy otherwise available.'

impeding of common law development the 'dark side' of the interaction between common law and statute.[45] My own view is that, in general, there should be no such dark side and that the common law should be developed in the normal way as the courts think appropriate subject to where such a common law development is expressly ruled out by the statute or would clash in whole or in part with the statutory regime.

Unfortunately, our courts have sometimes unnecessarily embraced this dark side. A classic illustration, which it took 25 years to correct, was the law on interest. Without running through all the details here, the story starts with the House of Lords' decision in 1893 in *London Chatham and Dover Rly Co* v. *South Eastern Rly,*[46] that interest could not be awarded as damages and that where a debt was unpaid the only remedy at common law was the award of the agreed sum. This meant that, unless interest was provided for in the contract, the creditor would be left out of pocket by the late payment of a debt. Not surprisingly, there were then statutory interventions culminating in section 35A of the Senior Courts Act 1981, which modified the law by allowing statutory interest to be awarded in certain situations. But could the common law be developed, by departing from *London Chatham and Dover Rly*, outside those specified statutory situations? That was the question confronting the House of Lords in 1985 in *President of India* v. *La Pintada Compania Navigacion SA.*[47] And it was answered in the

---

[45] Anne Davies, 'The Relationship between the Contract of Employment and Statute' in *The Contract of Employment* (general editor, Mark Freedland, Oxford, 2016) 73, 86.

[46] [1893] AC 429. [47] [1985] AC 104.

negative. It was held that the common law could not be developed to give damages as interest for failure to pay a debt because
the common law was regarded as having been frozen by section
35A of the Senior Courts Act 1981, which allowed the award of
interest in certain situations only.[48] This reasoning rested on the
false premise that, because Parliament had taken one step, it had
positively decided that no other development was permitted.
It was not until 2008 that a more enlightened House of Lords in
Sempra Metals Ltd v. *Inland Revenue Commissioners*[49] finally
accepted that statute had not frozen the common law in this
area, *London Chatham and Dover Rly Co* and *La Pintada* were
overruled, and it was recognised that damages can be awarded as
interest, including compound interest,[50] for failure to pay a debt.

---

[48] In Lord Brandon's words, giving the leading speech, at 130: '[W]hen
Parliament has given effect by legislation to some recommendations of
the Law Commission in a particular field, but has taken what appears to
be a policy decision not to give effect to a further such recommendation,
any decision of your Lordships' House which would have the result of
giving effect, by another route, to the very recommendation which
Parliament appears to have taken that policy decision to reject, could
well be regarded as an unjustifiable usurpation by your Lordships' House
of the functions which belong properly to Parliament.'

[49] [2007] UKHL 34, [2008] 1 AC 561. The actual decision in the case was not
concerned with damages as such: rather, it was that compound interest
can be awarded as a restitutionary remedy to reverse an unjust
enrichment.

[50] Although there remains a difficult question as to whether, in a case where
s. 35A of the Supreme Court Act 1981 applies and would allow the award
of simple interest only, there is an unacceptable clash if compound
interest may be awarded under *Sempra Metals*: see Andrew Burrows,
'Interest' in *Commercial Remedies: Resolving Controversies* (eds.
Graham Virgo and Sarah Worthington, Cambridge, 2017) 247, 268–271.

Another example, which has provoked a very heated debate among employment lawyers, is the law established in cases such as *Johnson* v. *Unisys Ltd*[51] and *Eastwood* v. *Magnox Electric plc*.[52] The essential question is whether the unfair dismissal legislation has frozen the development of the common law on damages for breach of the contract of employment by the manner of the dismissal. In *Johnson* v. *Unisys*, the House of Lords (Lord Steyn dissenting) held that it should not develop the common law so as to allow wrongful dismissal damages for mental distress or a psychiatric illness, or we might add pecuniary loss of reputation, contrary to the earlier restrictive decision in *Addis* v. *Gramophone Co*,[53] because to do so would undermine the special statutory compensation scheme for unfair dismissal. Their Lordships reasoned that to allow employees to recover damages beyond the salary that they were owed, and were not paid, for the notice period would conflict with that statutory scheme. In particular, had the claimant sued for unfair dismissal, the statutory maximum sum that he could at that time have recovered was £11,000 whereas he was claiming damages for loss of earnings of £400,000. In the words of Lord Nicholls:

> [A] common law right embracing the manner in which an employee is dismissed cannot satisfactorily co-exist with the statutory right not to be unfairly dismissed. A newly developed common law right of this nature, covering the same ground as the statutory right, would fly in the face of the limits Parliament has already prescribed on matters

---

[51] [2001] UKHL 13, [2003] 1 AC 518.
[52] [2004] UKHL 35, [2004] 3 WLR 322. [53] [1909] AC 488.

such as the classes of employees who have the benefit of the statutory right, the amount of compensation payable and the short time limits for making claims.[54]

Although one can see the force of this, the better view, in line with Lord Steyn's dissent, is that the courts should have developed the common law and that this would not have undermined the statutory unfair dismissal regime. The statutory unfair dismissal legislation can sit perfectly well with a full common law regime for damages for the manner of a wrongful dismissal. They can be viewed as simply concurrent causes of action, albeit that only employment tribunals, and not the courts, have jurisdiction in respect of unfair, as opposed to wrongful, dismissal. Any idea that the purpose of the unfair dismissal legislation was to halt the development of normal contractual rights is a false reading of history: the aim was to add protection to employees not to freeze their contractual rights.

I now turn to the third and final question within this second part of this lecture.

---

[54] [2001] UKHL 13, [2003] 1 AC 518 at [2]. For powerful criticism of this approach, see Lord Steyn in *Eastwood* v. *Magnox Electric plc* [2004] UKHL 35, [2004] 3 WLR 322 in which the House of Lords distinguished *Johnson* v. *Unisys* – as involving a wrongful dismissal as opposed to the breach of an employment contract distinct from wrongful dismissal – without reopening its correctness. Lord Nicholls recognised that carving out this '*Johnson* exclusion area' was unsatisfactory. He said, at [33], 'It goes without saying that the interrelation between the common law and statute having these awkward and unfortunate consequences is not satisfactory ... This situation merits urgent attention by the government and the legislature.' See also *Edwards* v. *Chesterfield Royal Hospital NHS Foundation Trust* [2011] UKSC 58, [2012] 2 AC 22.

What is the Impact on the Removal of the Common Law of Applying the 'Principle of Legality' in Interpreting a Statute?[55]

As explained and applied in, for example, *R* v. *Home Secretary, ex p Simms*,[56] which concerned the legality of prison rules banning prisoners from being interviewed by journalists, the principle of legality may be seen as a presumption of statutory interpretation. The principle requires that legislation, whether primary or secondary, should, if possible, be interpreted so as not to remove fundamental common law rights. The idea is that, given how unlikely it is that a statutory purpose would be to take away a fundamental common law right, that interpretation should only be adopted if the words clearly take away the right, whether expressly or by necessary implication. So analogously to 'conforming interpretation' under section 3 of the Human Rights Act 1998,[57] this common law principle of legality

---

[55] For excellent analyses of the principle of legality from an Australian perspective, see Dan R. Meagher, 'The Common Law Principle of Legality in the Age of Rights' (2011) *Melbourne Law Review* 449; and Michelle Sanson, *Statutory Interpretation* (2nd edn, Oxford, 2016) ch. 11.

[56] [2000] 2 AC 115. See especially Lord Steyn at 130 and Lord Hoffmann at 131. See also, e.g., *R* v. *Lord Chancellor, ex p Witham* [1998] QB 575 (where Laws J held that the right of access to the courts is a 'constitutional right' that a statute can take away only by express words or possibly by necessary implication); *R* v. *Sec of State for the Home Department, ex p Pierson* [1998] AC 539 per Lord Browne-Wilkinson at 573–575 (statutory discretion could not be lawfully exercised so as to infringe the 'basic' common law right not to have a sentence increased).

[57] See above, pp. 11–13. See generally, Sir Philip Sales, 'A Comparison of the Principle of Legality and Section 3 of the Human Rights Act 1998' (2009)

requires the courts to read down legislation, so far as possible, to be consistent with fundamental common law rights; and Executive action will be declared, or quashed, as unlawful if it infringes such rights. Although a matter of statutory interpretation, we can see that, as Lord Hoffmann pointed out in *Simms*, it is through this principle of legality and its protection of fundamental common law rights that the English common law recognises 'principles of constitutionality',[58] which elsewhere might be found in a written constitution: hence the excitement of the legality principle for constitutional lawyers.

The constitutional importance of this legality principle can be well illustrated by many cases,[59] but here I shall just pick

---

125 *Law Quarterly Review* 598; Alison Young, *Democratic Dialogue and the Constitution* (Oxford, 2017) 245–254.

[58] [2000] 2 AC 115, 131. In thinking about constitutional principles, we might also refer to the idea that certain statutes are 'constitutional statutes' which require express repeal and are not subject to an implied later repeal. See, e.g., Laws LJ's judgment in *Thorburn* v. *Sunderland CC* [2002] EWHC 195 (Admin), [2003] QB 151. See also *R (HS2 Action Alliance Ltd)* v. *Secretary of State for Transport* [2014] UKSC 3, [2014] 1 WLR 324, esp. at [207]–[208] (potential conflict between two constitutional statutes, the Bill of Rights and European Communities Act 1972). The link between constitutional statutes and the principle of legality is drawn by Farrah Ahmed and Adam Perry, 'Constitutional Statutes' (2017) 37 *Oxford Journal of Legal Studies* 461, 463.

[59] Indeed, while in *R (Privacy International)* v. *Investigatory Powers Tribunal* [2017] EWCA Civ 1868, the particular ouster clause was held, as a matter of statutory interpretation, to be effective in ousting judicial review of the decisions of the Investigatory Powers Tribunal, it was accepted, at [21], that the principle of legality underpins the restrictive interpretation of statutory provisions ousting the jurisdiction of the courts, exemplified by the reading down of the ouster clause, so as not to

two recent and controversial decisions of the Supreme Court in which the principle of legality was applied to quash Executive action as not being permitted by the relevant statute. First, in *R (on the application of Evans)* v. *Attorney-General*,[60] the question at issue was whether, in response to a freedom of information request, the letters of Prince Charles to Ministers (the so-called 'black-spider letters') should be made public. A court, the Upper Tribunal, ruled that that request should be granted. But the Attorney-General, applying section 53 of the Freedom of Information Act 2000 allowing him to issue a certificate denying disclosure 'on reasonable grounds', subsequently issued a certificate denying the request. By a majority (5–2), the Supreme Court held that the Attorney-General's issuing of that certificate was unlawful; and three of the five majority Justices (Lords Neuberger, Kerr and Reed) reasoned that this was because, although the statutory wording appeared to allow the Attorney-General to override the court's decision, that would contradict the fundamental common law right that the decision of a court could not be overridden by the Executive. Secondly, in *R (on the application of Unison)* v. *Lord Chancellor*[61] the Supreme

---

oust judicial review, in the seminal case of *Anisminic Ltd* v. *Foreign Compensation Commission* [1969] 2 AC 147.

[60] [2015] UKSC 21, [2015] AC 1787. See, generally, on this case, T.R. Allen, 'Law, Democracy and Constitutionalism: Reflections on *Evans* v. *A-G*' [2016] *Cambridge Law Journal* 38.

[61] [2017] UKSC 51, [2017] 3 WLR 409. This case neatly illustrates a general point that the principle of legality is more likely to have an impact in challenging delegated legislation rather than primary legislation. If exactly the same fees had been introduced by primary legislation, and an affected person had sought a declaration that the fees were unlawful, the primary legislation could probably not have been read down (leaving aside any EU

Court held that the Lord Chancellor's order, requiring pre-scribed fees to be paid for bringing proceedings in employment tribunals, was unlawful because, inter alia, it infringed what Lord Reed, giving the leading judgment, described as the common law 'constitutional right' of access to justice, without there being clear statutory wording permitting this. In other words, the statute permitting the Lord Chancellor's fee order did not expressly, or by necessary implication, permit fees to be set at such a level as to pose a real risk that people would in effect be prevented from exercising their right to access employment tribunals.

There are several difficult issues on this principle of legality, including, most obviously, what counts as a fundamental common law right as opposed to a common law right (clearly, not all common law rights are protected by the principle, for example, the common law right to restitution of a mistaken payment); and how far, if at all, do fundamental common law rights differ from what the Supreme Court in the *Unison* case labelled 'constitutional rights' (an attractive view on this is that they are synonymous). However, I here want to confine my remarks to one simple but important point. This is that, while the principle of legality is similar to what I looked at earlier in relation to the removal, or freezing, of the common law by statute, the two are distinct. Using the language of a statutory

point) so as to quash or reduce the fees as this would have directly contradicted the express statutory language. But where, as was the case, the primary legislation merely empowered the fixing of fees by the Lord Chancellor, the language left more scope for reading down to ensure that those fees did not infringe the common law right of access to the courts.

interpretative presumption, it may well be helpful and accurate to say, as a general proposition, that there is a presumption that the common law has not been removed or frozen.[62] But – and this is the important point of distinction – that presumption can be relatively easily displaced as a matter of ordinary statutory interpretation. In contrast, the 'principle of legality' engenders a strong presumption so that fundamental common law rights can be removed only by express words or by necessary implication.

[62] That there should be such a presumption might be said to reflect the common law's long historic development, which indicates that the common law should not be removed lightly. Much more problematic, in an age of statutes, is the notion that there is a wider presumption that a statute does not affect or change the common law. For such a presumption, see *R* v. *Morris* (1867) LR 1 CCR 90, 95 where Byles J said, 'It is a sound rule to construe a statute in conformity with common law rather than against it, except where or so far as the statute is plainly intended to alter the course of the common law.' See also *Greene* v. *Associated Newspapers Ltd* [2005] 1 All ER 30 at [61]–[66] (per Brooke LJ). See generally Daniel Greenberg, *Craies on Legislation* (11th edn, Sweet & Maxwell, 2017) para. 14.1.7 and 14.1.11; John Burrows, 'The Interrelation between Common Law and Statute' (1976) 3 *Otago Law Review* 583, 592–594. Roscoe Pound, 'Common Law and Legislation' (1908) 21 *Harvard Law Review* 383 warned against the judiciary treating statutes as inferior to the common law: while he accepted the importance of the principle of legality, this led Pound to reject as outdated any presumption of statutory interpretation that a statute is not intended to affect or change the common law. (For similar sentiments, see Justice Harlan Stone's famous statement in 'The Common Law in the United States' (1936) 50 *Harvard Law Review* 4, 15 that, contrary to the traditional view, a statute should not be viewed 'as an alien intruder in the house of the common law but a guest to be welcomed and made at home there'.) But less clear-cut, and not dealt with by Pound, is the position as to the general removal or freezing of the common law.

An excellent example of that important distinction being drawn is provided by Sir John Dyson's judgment in *R (Child Poverty Action Group)* v. *Secretary of State for Work and Pensions*.[63] Here a public authority had mistakenly overpaid social security payments. There was a statutory scheme laid down in section 71 of the Social Security Administration Act 1992 governing the repayment of such overpayments, which in some significant respects differed from the common law on restitution of mistaken payments. The question at issue, fitting alongside cases like the *Marcic* and *Total Network* cases that I have already looked at, was whether that statutory regime was exclusive or not. The Supreme Court held that indeed it was exclusive so that any claim by the public authority at common law had been removed. The judgments touch on a number of interesting issues on statutory interpretation but the important point for my present purposes is that Sir John Dyson made clear that the removal of the public authority's common law right to restitution of a mistaken payment did not involve the removal of a *fundamental* common law right. Therefore, the principle of legality,[64] applicable to the removal of fundamental common law rights, was not here

---

[63] [2010] UKSC 54, [2011] 2 AC 15.

[64] Sir John Dyson treated as part of, or alongside, the principle of legality, that certain basic tenets of the common law should not be regarded as having been overridden by statute: e.g. that legal professional privilege should be respected (*R (on the application of Morgan Grenfell & Co Ltd)* v. *Special Comr of Income Tax* [2002] UKHL 21, [2003] 1 AC 563) or that a crime requires mens rea (*B* v. *DPP* [2000] 2 AC 428).

in play, so that what he termed the 'high hurdle'[65] of the removal having to be express, or by necessary implication, did not apply.

3 Should Reform of the Common Law be by Judicial Development or by Statute?

The final issue I want to consider is the most debated of all in respect of the interaction of common law and statute: how far do we want the judges to reform and develop the common law or, on the contrary, should this be a matter for the Legislature? This raises central questions about the extent of judicial power.

The starting point is the recognition that judges, through their decisions, have created and updated the common law. In the past, this truth was suppressed by the fiction that somehow the judges were not themselves developing the law but were merely finding and declaring the true law that had always existed. One of the great turning points in our law was the denunciation of this as a 'fairy-tale' by Lord Reid in his brilliant lecture to the Society of Public Teachers of Law (now the Society of Legal Scholars) in 1971.[66]

But once we accept that appellate judges can and do make law by developing the common law, the difficult question is what are the limits, if any, of that creative power,

---

[65] [2010] UKSC 54, [2011] 2 AC 15, at [31]. See also, e.g., *Gifford* v. *Strang Patrick Stevedoring Pty Ltd* (2003) 214 CLR 269 at [36]–[37] (per McHugh J).

[66] 'The Judge as Lawmaker' (1972) 12 *Journal of the Society of Public Teachers of Law* 22.

which, it is important to stress, allows retrospective law-making by an unelected judiciary. Lord Goff in his wonderful speech in *Woolwich Equitable Building Society* v. *Inland Revenue Commissioners,*[67] in which the common law of unjust enrichment was developed to allow restitution as of right from a public authority that had obtained payments ultra vires, said that while he was aware of the boundary line, he was never very sure where to find it. Lord Goff pointed out that if judges had held back, we would not have had the modern tort of negligence or freezing injunctions or the modern law of judicial review. One can add that we would also not have had other famous examples of common law development, such as the removal of the rule that a husband cannot rape his wife,[68] or the award of mental distress damages in contract,[69] or the removal of the mistake of law bar to restitution in the law of unjust enrichment.[70]

Even confining ourselves to cases over the last ten years, there have been a number of Supreme Court decisions in which the courts have had to deal with this issue.[71] They

---

[67] [1993] AC 70.

[68] *R* v. *R* [1991] 2 All ER 597, CA; upheld [1992] 1 AC 599, HL. This was not a pure common law development because rape was defined by statute in the Sexual Offences (Amendment) Act 1976 s. 1(1). See generally, Andrew Burrows, 'Common Law Retrospectivity' in *Judge and Jurist* (eds. Andrew Burrows, David Johnston, and Reinhard Zimmermann, Oxford, 2013) 543, 551–556.

[69] *Jarvis* v. *Swan's Tours Ltd* [1973] QB 233.

[70] *Kleinwort Benson Ltd* v. *Lincoln City Council* [1999] 2 AC 349.

[71] In addition to these examples, in each of which there was at least some reference to the respective roles of the courts and Parliament, see, e.g., *Willers* v. *Joyce* [2016] UKSC 43, [2016] 3 WLR 477, extending the tort of

include the following in which the common law was developed: *Jones* v. *Kernott*[72] dealing with the property rights in their home of unmarried co-habitees; *Jones* v. *Kaney*[73] removing witness immunity in the tort of negligence; *R* v. *Jogee*[74] cutting back the scope of joint liability in criminal law; *Knauer* v. *Ministry of Justice*[75] deciding that the multiplier in calculating damages in fatal accident cases should run from the date of trial not the date of death; and *Patel* v. *Mirza*[76] favouring a 'range of factors' to fixed rules in relation to the defence of illegality. Going the other way, with the Supreme Court saying, inter alia, that any reform was a matter for Parliament, have been, for example, *R (on the application of Prudential plc)* v. *Special Commr of Income Tax*[77] in which it was decided that legal professional privilege should not be extended to include accountants giving legal advice; and *Michael* v. *Chief Constable of South Wales Police*[78] in which it was held that the police should have no

malicious prosecution to civil proceedings; *Armes* v. *Nottinghamshire County Council* [2017] UKSC 60, extending vicarious liability so that local authority are held liable for sexual abuse by foster parents.

[72] [2011] UKSC 53, [2012] 1 AC 776, esp. at [57], [78].

[73] [2011] UKHL 13, [2011] 2 AC 39, esp. at [128], [173], [190].

[74] [2016] UKSC 8, [2017] AC 387, esp. at [85].

[75] [2016] UKSC 9, [2016] AC 908, esp. at [26].

[76] [2016] UKSC 42, [2017] AC 467, esp. at [114].

[77] [2013] UKSC 1, [2013] 2 AC 185. The relevant passages are at [52], [61]–[67] (per Lords Neuberger and Walker), [81] (per Lord Hope), [101] (per Lord Reed). Lord Mance was also in the majority. Lords Sumption and Clarke dissented.

[78] [2015] UKSC 2, [2015] AC 1732. The relevant passage of Lord Toulson's leading judgment is at [130]. Lady Hale and Lord Kerr dissented. See generally, Stelios Tofaris and Sandy Steel, 'Negligence Liability for Omissions and the Police' [2016] *Cambridge Law Journal* 128.

liability in the tort of negligence where they had failed to respond to a 999 call from a woman who was murdered shortly afterwards by her former partner.

Where the boundary should be drawn has been analysed at a high level of generality by many of the great figures in jurisprudence but also, at a more practical level, by a number of English judges. These include our Chair for this lecture,[79] building on an influential analysis by the late Lord Bingham[80] who suggested that particular caution

---

[79] Lord Dyson, 'Where the Common Law Fears to Tread' (2013) 34 *Statute Law Review* 1: he regarded Lord Bingham's propositions (i) (iii) and (iv) as relatively uncontroversial and therefore concentrated on propositions (ii) and (v). See similarly the lecture given by Lord Dyson, 'Are the judges too powerful?' (UCL Bentham Association Presidential Address 2014). I am not convinced that there is any difference between Lord Bingham's points (iii) and (v). In so far as point (v) is referring to institutional incompetence, outside controversial issues of social policy (and leaving aside where Parliament has entrusted matters to the discretion of a public authority), it is hard to see where (v) bites and where it does not. Lord Dyson gives as a possible example vicarious liability in the context of *Morgans* v. *Launchbury* [1973] AC 127. However, through their legal expertise and experience, judges are in a very good position to make decisions on vicarious liability (and that is not a controversial issue of social policy where there are sensitive moral/political choices to be made). Lord Dyson also makes the point that the adversarial system might conceivably mean that the judges are not given all the best information to make decisions. But one can counter-argue that this is increasingly rare and does not predominantly occur in any particular class of case. And if the judges get it wrong, Parliament can always reverse what they have done.

[80] Tom Bingham, 'The Judge as Lawmaker: an English Perspective' in *The Business of Judging: Selected Essays and Speeches* (Oxford, 2000) 25–34. See also, e.g., Justice Michael Kirby, *Judicial Activism* (Hamlyn Lectures 2003); Lord Walker, 'Developing the Common Law: How Far is

should be exercised by the judiciary in the following five situations: (i) where citizens have reasonably ordered their affairs relying on a certain understanding of the law; (ii) where reform calls for a detailed legislative code; (iii) where the question involves an issue of controversial social policy; (iv) where the issue is already being considered by the Legislature; and (v) where the issue is far removed from ordinary judicial experience.

These guidelines are helpful but, in applying them, I would suggest that there are four further important considerations to bear in mind.[81] I am also assuming that,

Too Far?' (2013) 37 *Melbourne University Law Review* 232, esp. 250–253; Lady Hale, 'Legislation or judicial law reform: where should judges fear to tread?' SLS Annual Conference in Oxford, 7 September 2016 (available on the Supreme Court's website).

[81] A different way of thinking about where the boundary should be drawn is to think of the relative advantages and disadvantages of legislative as against judicial law reform. So the advantages of legislative law reform include that: one can deal with a wide area in precisely the way one wishes; there is no need to wait for a particular case to reach the highest court; the change can be, and almost always is, non-retrospective; the reform can be fully informed by differing points of view, research and consultation; and difficult decisions are ultimately legitimised because the process can be seen to reflect the democratic will. In contrast, the disadvantages of legislative law reform as against judicial law reform include that: it is difficult to find time in the legislative programme for 'non-sexy' technical law reform; there is a danger of legislation freezing the law so that 'mistakes' cannot be corrected so easily or, perhaps expressed more accurately, the law cannot be so easily adapted to changing circumstances and values; the very process of a bill going through Parliament can undermine and complicate its drafting and structure thereby producing law that is irrational and incoherent; and legislation can produce a clash between the common law and the statutory inroad which may produce costly and problematic demarcation issues.

following on my earlier discussion, the development of the common law would not clash with any statutory regime.

First, under the UK constitutional position, there is a fundamental principle of Parliamentary sovereignty. It is not in doubt that the UK Parliament can reverse whatever the courts do and the courts cannot strike down that legislation as unconstitutional. The democratic will through Parliament can always override what the courts have done. Professor Mark Elliott makes this point very succinctly: '[T]he very existence of Parliamentary sovereignty might be considered to remove the sting from certain criticisms of judicial activism ... since the sovereignty doctrine ensures that, any such activism notwithstanding, Parliament retains the final word.'[82]

Secondly, very commonly, the issues in relation to the development of the common law are not ones that the Legislature is going to take forward. Time for legislation is tight. Normally, law reform of this type is not a vote winner. So if the courts do not take forward the reform, that usually means in practice that that is the end of it. In other words, it is disingenuous to say 'Reform is better left to Parliament' when in reality it is almost certain that Parliament will do nothing.

Thirdly, it is useful, in my view, to think of a sliding scale from what Lord Reid in *Pettitt* v. *Pettitt*[83] called 'lawyer's law' through to law involving controversial social policy choices. The courts, being unelected and therefore without

---

[82] Judicial Power Project Blog entitled 'Judicial Power: A Response to Professor Finnis'.

[83] [1970] AC 777, 795.

any direct democratic mandate, should exercise greater restraint as they reach the higher end of that scale. Other people have preferred to describe the important distinction as one between principle and policy (or between non-polycentric and polycentric issues). Some, for example, Professor Robert Stevens,[84] have argued that there is a rigid line between principle and policy; and that is the clear boundary the courts should not cross. That seems to me misconceived. There is no sharp distinction between principle and policy.[85] Courts generally have to take both into account in developing the common law. For example, in the law of tort, in deciding on whether a duty of care is owed in a novel case, in addition to relevant principles of reasonable care and reasonable foreseeability, policies such as the fear of floodgates, or undermining individual responsibility, or concerns about encouraging defensive practices or outflanking a contractual allocation of risk between the parties or unduly

---

[84] *Torts and Rights* (Oxford, 2007) esp. ch. 14.

[85] For similar views to mine, that both principle and policy are important in understanding, e.g., the law of tort, see Jane Stapleton, 'Duty of Care and Economic Loss: A Wider Agenda' (1991) 107 *Law Quarterly Review* 249; Jane Stapleton, 'Duty of Care Factors: A Selection from the Judicial Menus' in *The Law of Obligations* (eds. Peter Cane and Jane Stapleton, Clarendon, 1998) 59; Andrew Robertson, 'Justice, Community Welfare and the Duty of Care' (2011) 127 *Law Quarterly Review* 370; Andrew Robertson, 'Rights, Pluralism and the Duty of Care' in Donal Nolan and Andrew Robertson, *Rights and Private Law* (Hart, 2012) 435–458; Jeff King, 'The Pervasiveness of Polycentricity' (2008) *Public Law* 101; Jeff King, 'Institutional Approaches to Judicial Restraint' (2008) 28 *Oxford Journal of Legal Studies* 409, esp. 414–422. See also James Plunkett, 'Principle and Policy in Private Law Reasoning' [2016] *Cambridge Law Journal* 366.

interfering with a public authority's discretionary powers, are all legitimately relevant. These elements of policy do not involve controversial social policy choices and are well within the competence of the judiciary.

The fourth additional consideration is the traditional common law technique centred on precedent. This is characterised not by giant leaps but by incremental steps that, in most cases, have been anticipated in previous case law. Provided a judge respects these constraints of the common law technique – and, if applicable, the rules of precedent including the 1966 Practice Statement – it may be thought that there is little to fear from judicial law reform because these constraints prevent a judge starting afresh by imposing his or her own preferred political views. In other words, while the judges may be regarded in some cases as making law, provided they act within the traditional constraints they are not acting as mini-legislators. The traditional development of the common law is significantly different than legislating. The common law develops incrementally so that, in contrast to legislators, the historical institutional tradition acts as a severe constraint on what the judges can do.[86]

Applying Lord Bingham's guidelines, with those four further considerations in mind,[87] my view is that it

---

[86] This is emphasised by John Gardner in 'Legal Positivism: 5 ½ Myths' in *Law as a Leap of Faith* (Oxford, 2012) 19–53, esp. 37–42.

[87] We might add as a fifth consideration that the judges have by and large done a good job in developing the common law. We entrust them to do this because they have proved themselves to be good at it. Indeed, we might argue that, if the common law was not thought to be good law, it would have disappeared by now. It is not at all surprising that, in

should in practice be rare for the Supreme Court to decline to adopt a particular development of the common law that it otherwise believes to be appropriate on the ground that the development is better left to Parliament.[88] This is not to say that, in practice, there is no boundary. It is clear, for example, that, not least because of the intense objection to retrospective punishment[89] – and common law reform is almost inevitably retrospective[90] – the courts should not develop the

developing lawyers' law, the judges, as some of our very best lawyers, do an excellent job because the development involves a mastery of complex legal issues. But even where judges are pushing out from very legalistic decisions towards controversial decisions of social policy, it is strongly arguable that their collective legal experience means that they have particularly well-informed insights on some of the policy choices required so that, in many cases, there is no need to rely just on a democratically elected body to make those choices.

[88] For a similar approach, see my article, 'The Relationship between Common Law and Statute in the Law of Obligations' (2012) 128 *Law Quarterly Review* 232, 247–248. It is important to stress that I was there arguing that, in the context of the law of obligations and provided the judges are deploying traditional incremental reasoning rather than making a wide-ranging social policy choice, it should be rare for them to refuse to develop the common law in deference to legislative reform. Cf. James Lee, 'The Doctrine of Precedent and the Supreme Court' (Inner Temple Lecture, April 2011) 2, 17–18.

[89] An additional factor is that new crimes need to be supported by a regime of rules concerning the type of offence and possible sentences that the courts are not in a position to lay down.

[90] On the possibility of prospective overruling, see *Re Spectrum Plus Ltd* [2005] UKHL 41, [2005] 2 AC 680. Cf. *Royal Bank of Scotland plc v. Etridge* (No 2) [2001] UKHL 44, [2002] 2 AC 773; Dame Mary Arden, 'Prospective Overruling' (2004) 120 *Law Quarterly Review* 7.

common law to add new crimes.[91] There may also be occasional cases in which the courts are asked to develop the common law, especially involving family law, where, on the scale I have referred to, the issue is so much at the top end away from lawyer's law that the courts should be inclined not to change the law.[92] This may be said to underpin, for

---

[91] *Knuller (Publishing, Printing and Promotions) Ltd* v. *DPP* [1973] AC 435. Cf. *Shaw* v. *DPP* [1962] AC 220.

[92] Rather than being a development of the common law, these questions of controversial social policy (e.g. whether civil partnership should extend to opposite-sex couples, which was the issue in *Steinfeld* v. *Secretary of State for Education* [2017] EWCA Civ 81, [2017] 3 WLR 1237) are more likely to come before the courts for a decision as to whether legislation is incompatible with the Human Rights Act 1998. But even though the courts have expressly been given the power to adopt a (strained) conforming interpretation (s. 3) or to make a declaration of incompatibility (s. 4), we would expect them to tread very carefully in relation to such questions (unless the incompatibility with a convention right is clear-cut as it was in the early cases of *Bellinger* v. *Bellinger* [2003] UKHL 21 (on the right to marry of transsexuals) and *Ghaidan* v. *Godin-Mendoza* [2004] UKHL 30, [2004] 2 AC 557 (on the tenancy rights of same-sex partners)). As Lord Reed said in *R (Nicklinson)* v. *Ministry of Justice* [2014] UKSC 38, [2015] AC 657, at [297], 'The issue raises highly controversial questions of social policy . . . [It] therefore requires Parliament to be allowed a wide margin of judgment . . . that is not to say that the courts lack jurisdiction . . . But it means that the courts should attach very considerable weight to Parliament's assessment.' In that case, it was held by a five to four majority that the blanket ban on assisted suicide under the Suicide Act 1961 s. 2 is incompatible with Article 8 of the ECHR. But of the majority, only Lady Hale and Lord Kerr would have gone ahead and immediately made a declaration of incompatibility: Lords Neuberger, Mance and Wilson preferred to defer making such a declaration until the Legislature had had a chance to consider the matter. The minority (Lords Sumption, Clarke, Reed and Hughes) reasoned that the courts should not make such a declaration because, inter alia, it was a matter raising

example, Lord Neuberger's dissenting reasoning in *Stack v. Dowden*[93] on co-ownership between cohabitees where he said that reform of the law in this area was for Parliament, and Lady Hale's approach in *Radmacher v. Granatino*[94] to the question whether ante-nuptial agreements should be recognised as legally binding contracts in which she said that that was a matter for Parliament, albeit that in both those cases we can powerfully counter-argue that the questions did not themselves go beyond lawyer's law to require a controversial decision of social policy. But that can certainly not be said of *R (Nicklinson)*

a fundamental moral and social dilemma on which Parliament had already made a choice. Lords Sumption, Clarke and Hughes came close to saying that the courts were institutionally incompetent to make such a decision. See also, subsequent to the debates in Parliament rejecting the Falconer Bill on assisted suicide, *R (Conway) v. Secretary of State for Justice* [2017] EWHC 2447 (Admin), [2017] HRLR 14, in which the Divisional Court held that, in the context of a person with motor-neurone disease seeking help to commit suicide, the Suicide Act 1961 s. 2 was compatible with Article 8 of the ECHR: taking into account the discretionary judgment that should be afforded to Parliament, the prohibition on assistance was necessary to protect the weak and vulnerable. On the general question of the interrelationship between ss. 3 and 4, arguing that s. 4 should be more liberally used at the expense of s. 3, see Shona Wilson Stark, 'Facing Facts: Judicial Approaches to Section 4 of the Human Rights Act 1998' (2017) 133 *Law Quarterly Review* 631. For an excellent recent example of a declaration of incompatibility being made under s. 4, where a conforming interpretation under s. 3 was not possible, see *Smith v. Lancashire Teaching Hospitals NHS Foundation Trust* [2017] EWCA Civ 1916, [2018] 2 WLR 1063 (Fatal Accidents Act 1976, s. 1A, in not allowing bereavement damages to be claimed by a long-term cohabitee of the deceased, held to be incompatible with Article 8 of the ECHR).

[93] [2007] UKHL 17, [2007] 2 AC 432.
[94] [2010] UKSC 42, [2011] 1 AC 534.

v. *Ministry of Justice*[95] in which the courts correctly decided that, at common law, there should be no development of necessity as a defence to murder so as to accommodate certain cases of euthanasia because that was a matter for Parliament. However, in the vast majority of cases, the Supreme Court should not hold back with incremental common law reform. It follows that, although the decisions in the *Prudential* and *Michael* cases not to develop the law may or may not have been correct (in my view, they were incorrect), that part of the reasoning in which the Supreme Court argued that any development was for Parliament, not the courts, was very disappointing. This is because those cases did not involve controversial issues of social policy, the developments in question would have required only incremental steps within the standard common law tradition, and none of Lord Bingham's other reasons for caution were in play.

---

[95] The common law arguments were dealt with in the Divisional Court (led by Toulson LJ), [2012] EWHC 2381 (Admin), and the Court of Appeal, [2013] EWCA Civ 961, but were not taken up to the Supreme Court which focussed purely on the Human Rights Act 1998 (see above note 92). Toulson LJ said that the matter was for Parliament not the courts. '[I]t is for Parliament to decide whether to change the law on euthanasia . . . The reasons have to do with competence, constitutionality, and control of the consequences . . . ' (at [75]). '[I]t is one thing for the courts to adapt and develop the principles of the common law incrementally in order to keep up with the requirements of justice in a changing society, but major changes involving matters of controversial social policy are for Parliament' (at [79]). He also rejected the Human Rights Act 1998 argument as 'these are matters for Parliament to decide' (at [150]).

Conclusion

The interaction of common law and statute raises central, fascinating and practically important issues many of which are rarely coherently analysed in our law schools. On the three main topics I have explored in this lecture, I have made the following groups of arguments:

(i) It is entirely appropriate for the courts to develop the common law by analogy to statutes. To deny this not only deprives the courts of a valuable resource for enriching the common law but also needlessly undermines the important goal of legal coherence, which dictates that, wherever possible, like cases should be treated alike.

(ii) Ordinary statutory interpretation determines whether a statute has removed an area of the common law or has frozen the common law's development. In deciding the difficult cases, the most important factor is whether the common law's co-existence or development clashes with the operation of the statute. In some past cases, the courts can be criticised for having been too ready to treat a statutory reform as freezing common law development. Closely linked to the general removal of the common law is the constitutionally exciting 'principle of legality' which protects fundamental common law rights and is the common law analogue of conforming interpretation under section 3 of the Human Rights Act 1998.

(iii) In the vast majority of cases – leaving aside particularly the creation of new crimes and decisions involving controversial questions of social policy – the

Supreme Court should not defer to Parliament by holding back from an incremental reform of the common law that it otherwise considers appropriate. After all, in our system, Parliamentary sovereignty constitutes the ultimate check on judicial power.

Lecture 3

Improving Statutes

Drawing on my experiences as a Law Commissioner for England and Wales,[1] my focus here is on the question: how might we improve the quality of our statute law?

All lawyers will have come across extremely complex and opaque statutory provisions. Perhaps the most dramatic expression of judicial exasperation with a statute is that of Lord Justice Harman in 1964 in *Davy* v. *Leeds Corporation.* Speaking of the provisions on compulsory purchase in the Town and Country Planning Act 1959, he said:[2]

---

[1] Without intending any disrespect to other Law Commissions, my references to the Law Commission are to the Law Commission for England and Wales.

[2] [1964] WLR 1218, 1124–1125; affd [1965] 1 WLR 445, HL. Sometimes a whole Act is the subject of judicial criticism. This was the fate of the Limitation Act 1963, which sensibly introduced a more flexible discoverability starting date for the running of time in personal injury cases but did so with drafting that muddied the basic concept. In *Central Asbestos Co Ltd* v. *Dodd* [1973] AC 518, 553, Lord Salmon summed up the general feeling of the courts when he said: 'This Act has been before the courts on many occasions during its comparatively short life. I do not think there are many judges who have had to consider it who have not criticised the wholly unnecessary complexity and deplorable obscurity of its language. It seems as if it was formulated to disguise rather than reveal the meaning which it was intended to bear.'

88

To reach a conclusion on this matter involved the court in wading through a monstrous legislative morass, staggering from stone to stone and ignoring the marsh gas exhaling from the forest of schedules lining the way on each side. I regarded it at one time, I must confess, as a slough of despond through which the court would never drag its feet but I have, by leaping from tussock to tussock as best I might, eventually, pale and exhausted, reached the other side.

In 2008, Mitting J at first instance in *R (Noone) v. Governor of Drake Hall Prison*[3] noted that it had taken almost five hours to explain to him the effect of some transitional provisions relating to a criminal sentence. When the case reached the Supreme Court, Lord Phillips said, 'Hell is a fair description of the problem of statutory interpretation caused by [these] transitional provisions.'[4] And in Lord Judge's words, 'It is outrageous that so much intellectual effort, as well as public time and resources, have had to be expended in order to discover a route through the legislative morass to what should be . . . the simplest and most certain of questions – the prisoner's release date.'[5]

More recently, I have spent many hours trying to understand aspects of the Consumer Rights Act 2015. This had as one of its aims to make the law clearer and simpler for consumers. If contract law professors are confused, one dreads

---

[3] [2008] EWHC 207 (Admin) at [1]. The provisions in question were in the Criminal Justice Act 2003 (Commencement No 8 and Transitional and Saving Provisions) Order 2005, SI 2005/950.

[4] [2010] UKSC 30, [2010] 1 WLR 1743, at [1]. [5] Ibid. at [87].

to think what the 'average consumer' (to quote a phrase from the Act) makes of it all.

However, as will become clear, my purpose in this lecture is certainly not to attack those who draft our statutes. On the contrary, I have huge respect for Parliamentary Counsel. One of the greatest pleasures of my career was working closely with them during my years at the Law Commission between 1994 and 1999. Far from 'knocking' them, one of my messages is that their role and work needs to be better known and appreciated than it now is.

With that by way of introduction, I divide up this lecture into four parts all concerned, even if loosely, with how statute law may be improved: (1) The style of statutory drafting. (2) The central role of Parliamentary Counsel. (3) The role of the Law Commission in respect of consolidation and statute repeals. (4) Pre- and post-legislative scrutiny.

Before I go any further, I should make two points clear. First I am not considering, and have insufficient experience to comment on, whether there is a need for any reform of the standard Parliamentary process and procedure, from first reading onwards, by which a bill becomes law. So, for example, it appears that late amendments can detrimentally affect the quality of our statutes. But, whether there is anything that can be done about that, is outside my remit tonight. Secondly, as in my earlier two lectures, I am focussing on primary legislation (i.e. statutes, Acts of Parliament) and not on secondary legislation (i.e. statutory instruments and the like).[6]

---

[6] I am also not looking at what Daniel Greenberg in 'Dangerous Trends in Modern Legislation' (2015) *Public Law* 96 has called 'quasi-legislation'.

So I am not examining the question,[7] which Brexit has brought to the forefront of attention, of whether too much power is being entrusted to the Executive through secondary legislation, in particular by the use of so-called Henry VIII powers.[8]

1 The Style of Statutory Drafting

In general, legislation in this jurisdiction is very detailed and aims to cover all possible eventualities that can be foreseen. It is often said that, in this respect, drafting in a common law system contrasts with drafting in civilian systems because the basic law in civilian systems derives from codes which tend to be drafted at the level of principle.[9] This contrast may

By this he means codes of conduct, guidance, directions and the like, which are drafted within departments, laid down by Ministers, and given the force of law by primary legislation, but which are never scrutinised by Parliament. Greenberg argues that this quasi-legislation poses serious constitutional dangers primarily because of the lack of scrutiny but also because it is often difficult to find.

[7] This has been examined by Lord Judge in several public lectures: see, especially, Lord Judge, 'Ceding Power to the Executive; the Resurrection of Henry VIII' (lecture on 12 April 2016 at King's College London); 'A Judge's View on the Rule of Law' (Annual Bingham Lecture, 3 May 2017).

[8] In general terms, these give Ministers the power in secondary legislation to amend primary legislation. For a careful analysis of exactly what is meant by a Henry VIII clause/power, see Lee Harvey, 'Delegating Legislative Power: From Modern Day Complexity to Henry VIII', *The Loophole*, October 2017, 27–36.

[9] Reinhard Zimmermann, '*Statuta Sunt Stricte Interpretanda*? Statutes and the Common Law: A Continental Perspective' [1997] *Cambridge Law*

exaggerate the position because the civil codes are filled in by more detailed statutes and, even in common law systems, we do of course have examples of legislative codes with high level drafting, such as the great commercial codes at the end of the nineteenth century on, for example, sale of goods and bills of exchange.[10] There are also plainly examples in this jurisdiction of statutes in particular areas that are drafted in terms of principle. One thinks, for example, of the Occupiers' Liability Acts 1957 and 1984, which essentially mirror the common law tort of negligence;[11] and, an even more important example, the Human Rights Act 1998.[12] But, in general, there does seem to

---

Journal 315 at 325–328; John Cartwright, *Contract Law: An Introduction to the English Law of Contract for the Civil Lawyer* (3rd edn, Hart, 2016) at 45: '[T]he drafting of statutes [in this jurisdiction] is much more detailed than in most civil law jurisdictions.' See, in particular, the excellent comparative analysis by Sir William Dale, *Legislative Drafting: A New Approach* (Butterworths, 1977), which compared drafting styles in the UK with France, Germany and Sweden.

[10] Sale of Goods Act 1893 (now Sale of Goods Act 1979); Bills of Exchange Act 1882.

[11] In *Roles* v. *Nathan* [1963] 1 WLR 1117 at 1122, Lord Denning MR, in praising the 1957 Act, cited its draftsman as saying, 'The Act would replace a principle of the common law with a new principle . . . instead of having [a] judgment . . . construed as if it were a statute, one is to have a statute which can be construed as if it were a judgment.' See generally on the 1957 and 1984 statutes, Stephen Bailey, 'Occupiers' Liability: the Enactment of "Common Law" Principles' in *Tort Law and the Legislature* (eds. T.T. Arvind and Jenny Steele, Hart, 2013) ch. 9.

[12] Other more recent examples of 'principled' drafting, where the reader can see a build-up of detail from the start of clear principle, as well as a clear map as to where the Act is going, include the Mental Capacity Act 2005 and the Banking Act 2009. See also, although just one section rather than a whole Act, s. 42 of the Gambling Act 2005 (on the offence of

be some validity in contrasting drafting in the civilian and common law worlds.

In 1975, the Renton Committee Report[13] recommended that, while perhaps not appropriate in all areas, in line with what the Committee regarded as the civilian style, 'encouragement should be given to [drafting by] the use of statements of principle, that is to say, the formulation of broad general rules'.[14]

Clearly statutory drafting has been significantly simplified and improved over the 40 years since the Renton Committee's recommendations. In general, statutes use more direct everyday language with shorter sentences and fewer sub-clauses than in the past.[15] There is greater attention given to clarifying the structure of the Act through headings and so-called 'overview clauses'.[16] And there has been the Tax

cheating at gambling which was examined in *Ivey* v. *Genting Casinos UK Ltd* [2017] UKSC 670, [2017] 3 WLR 1212). Although tax is clearly an area where ultimately detail may be crucial, the Tax Law Rewrite leading to, e.g., the Income Tax 2007 was a big improvement, in terms of principled drafting, on much of the previous tax legislation: see below p. 94.

[13] *The Preparation of Legislation*, Report of a Committee chaired by Sir David Renton (1975, Cmnd 6053) ('Renton Committee Report').

[14] Renton Committee Report, para. 10.13 and recommendation 13.

[15] Since 2014, as part of the so-called 'Good Law Initiative', the Office of Parliamentary Counsel has put up on its website a guide to drafting, which stresses that, wherever possible, simpler and more straightforward words and sentences and structure should be used with various helpful examples of this being given. Another general improvement is in the way that amendments to other legislation are set out: in general, they take the form of setting out the amended text (see below p. 110).

[16] See, e.g., the Banking Act 2009. See generally Daniel Greenberg, *Laying Down the Law* (Sweet & Maxwell, 2011) 260–261.

Law Rewrite, which, at least for a time,[17] went a long way not only to consolidating and amending tax legislation but also to making tax provisions more straightforward.

However, there is still, in my view, room for a shift of culture towards more principled drafting in this jurisdiction.[18] So, although paradoxically this requires more time not less, I would like to suggest that drafters, first, set out clearly the general rules and principles that are being laid down in a statute before going on, secondly, to consider very carefully indeed what level of detail is *really* needed in filling out those general rules. In particular, the beguiling temptation to tie down in detail all conceivable matters should be resisted because to do so produces needlessly complex provisions and will in any event inevitably fail because tying everything down is an impossible goal.

---

[17] For witnesses suggesting that standards have slipped over the last few years, see *The Legislative Process: Preparing Legislation for Parliament*, House of Lords Select Committee on the Constitution (25 October 2017, HL Paper 27) at paras. 114–115. This Report is hereinafter referred to as the Constitution Committee's 2017 Report on *Preparing Legislation*.

[18] This was also supported by Sir William Dale. But this suggestion was not agreed with by the Hansard Society, *Making the Law* (1992) at 61 who agreed with the view of Sir Patrick Mayhew, 'Can Legislation Ever be Simple, Clear, and Certain' (1990) 11 *Statute Law Review* 1, 7: 'I confess to great difficulty in seeing how a general statement of principle or purpose could enable the law to be developed by the judges, and thereby affect the public's rights, in a way foreseeable with sufficient accuracy by that public.' It has been suggested to me that it is difficult to amend the style of drafting where one is often amending previous statutes drafted in detailed form: but it is hard to see why this is an insuperable problem; if it were, the change to simpler more straightforward drafting over the last 40 years would not have occurred.

Moreover, as a guide to behaviour, striving to cover every last detail is counter-productive because it tends to render the statute impenetrable for citizens and legal advisers. Often we simply cannot see the wood for the trees.

In considering this, there is an important link to be made between the style of drafting and statutory interpretation. I explained in my first lecture that, in English law, there has been a shift over the last 50 years from a literal to a contextual and purposive approach to statutory interpretation. At a time when the predominant approach to statutory interpretation was more literal, one could understand that the style of drafting would seek to ensure that everything was explicitly tied down. This was because the dominant approach to interpretation left the courts with no real scope to go behind the literal meaning of words in order to effect the statute's purpose. But with the modern adoption of a purposive approach, and with an acceptance that statutes are always speaking, the style of drafting can be less detailed with more emphasis being placed on trusting the judges just as they are trusted to develop the common law.[19]

---

[19] Daniel Greenberg, 'All Trains Stop at Crewe: The Rise and Rise of Contextual Drafting' (2005) *European Journal of Law Reform* 31, 42–43. It has been suggested to me that, in terms of guiding behaviour, case law statutory interpretation is just as complex as detailed legislative provisions so that nothing is to be gained by drafting at the level of principle. I disagree. At least for legal advisers, and for citizens with sufficient time and interest to delve into the law, case law interpretation is, at least in general, easier to understand than detailed legislative provisions, not least because there is a real-life factual situation in play. In any event, judges in interpreting statutes – and in that sense fleshing out the detail – have the considerable advantage over the Legislature in having the benefit of hindsight.

In short, one can argue that our style of drafting has not entirely caught up with the reality that the predominant approach to statutory interpretation is now purposive not literal.

Several commentators have drawn the link between styles of drafting and the approach to interpretation.[20] For example, Professor Reinhard Zimmermann has written:

> Legal drafting and techniques of interpretation are usually inextricably interrelated. Rigidity in the interpretation of statutes in Republican Rome went hand in hand with the cautious, unabstract and clumsy punctiliousness with which their draftsman tried to provide for all kinds of eventualities.[21]

Zimmermann argued that, as in Republican Rome, so the drafting style in this jurisdiction, compared to that in Germany, is often needlessly detailed. One of the examples he gave of this struck a particular chord for me because it was part of a bill for which I had primary responsibility during my time at the Law Commission. This became section 2(4)–(7) of the Contracts (Rights of Third Parties) Act 1999. What that Act did was to reform the privity of contract doctrine by giving an expressly identified third party the right in certain circumstances to enforce a term of a contract to which it was not a party. Section 2 of the Act deals with how far, if at all, the contracting parties can change their minds so as to remove or alter that third party right by rescinding or varying the contract

---

[20] Reinhard Zimmermann, '*Statuta Sunt Stricte Interpretanda*? Statutes and the Common Law: A Continental Perspective' [1997] *Cambridge Law Journal* 315. See also the Law Commission, *The Interpretation of Statutes* (1969) para. 5; the Renton Committee Report para. 19.1.

[21] Ibid. at 325.

without the third party's consent. But the particular target of Zimmermann's criticism is that that section goes on to deal in detail, in four substantial subsections, with the situation where the third party's consent is or might be required but cannot be obtained because the third party cannot reasonably be located or is mentally incapable of giving consent.

Drawing on the German style of drafting, Zimmermann was of the view that such detail is unnecessary, and, in retrospect, I think he is absolutely correct.[22] It would have been better to have dealt with what is, in truth, a somewhat remote issue by saying that the third party's consent need not be obtained where impractical to do so and leaving it at that. The detail merely serves to make this section of the Act needlessly long and elaborate, tends to obscure the principle and is in any event non-comprehensive.[23]

Before moving on from the style of drafting, I would like to add a linked suggestion. This concerns the use of examples. One of the reasons statutes are so disliked by students compared to case law is that their application to facts in real

---

[22] See also John Cartwright, *Contract Law: An Introduction to the English Law of Contract for the Civil Lawyer* (3rd edn, Hart, 2016) at 44–47 where he compares s. 2 of the 1999 Act with the equivalent provisions in the French, German and Italian civil codes. When I look back at the 1999 Act, there are other sections that are susceptible to the same criticism. For example, the provisions in section 3 on defences available to the promisor are far more elaborate than necessary especially as, in relation to set off, they appear simply to lay down the law that would surely have been applied in any event.

[23] So, e.g., the subsections do not deal with where the location of the third party is known, but the contracting parties cannot reasonably make contact with him or her.

life is not spelt out. Case law is fun because we have a real-life situation at the forefront of attention.[24] With statutes, in contrast, we have abstract rules with no real-life facts to help and this makes their study and understanding dry and difficult. Most statutes would be made easier to understand for everyone if there were accompanying examples of how they are seen as applying.[25] After all, examples will usually have had to be thought about in order to perfect the drafting. Examples, of the type I have in mind, have occasionally been included in a statute. Perhaps the best known is the Consumer Credit Act 1974, which contains, in Schedule 2, 24 examples of the operation of the Act.[26] I am also conscious that what were referred to when I was at the Law Commission as 'new-style' Explanatory Notes – they were introduced in 1998–1999[27] – do sometimes contain examples.[28] These Explanatory Notes, written by the relevant Department – although arguably Parliamentary Counsel ought to be given a bigger role in their drafting – accompany first a bill and

---

[24] See above p. 46.

[25] See the Renton Committee Report p. 58 and recommendation 9 favouring the greater use of examples. See generally on the use of examples, Daniel Greenberg, *Craies on Legislation* (11th edn, Sweet & Maxwell, 2017) para. 8.1.10; Ross Carter, 'Statutory Interpretation Using Legislative Examples: Bennion on Multiple Consumer Credit Agreements' (2011) *Statute Law Review* 86, esp. at 90.

[26] See also, e.g., the Income Tax Act 2007, which has worked examples.

[27] See *Parliament and the Legislative Process* (2004), a Report by the Select Committee on the Constitution, chaired by Lord Norton (hereinafter referred to as the 'Norton Committee Report'), at para. 78.

[28] See, e.g., Marriage (Same Sex Couples) Act 2013, Explanatory Notes 28 and 35.

then an Act and, if properly formulated, should contain valuable information about the purpose[29] and history of the Act and how the different provisions are seen as operating. It has been clearly established that Explanatory Notes can be taken into consideration by the courts in interpreting

---

[29] There has been some debate over the years as to whether a statute should contain, in a section at its start, a statement of its purpose or purposes (a so-called 'purpose clause'). The Renton Committee recommended that such clauses should be more widely used: Renton Committee Report para. 11.8 and recommendation 15. For the contrary view, see Hansard Society, *Making the Law* (1992) paras. 241–242. Both reports refer to the concerns of Parliamentary Counsel that such a statement of purpose may cause confusion by clashing with the later details in the Act (but surely that ought to be avoidable by careful drafting). For rare examples of such clauses, see, e.g., Banking Act 2009, s. 1; Finance Act 2013, s. 206. My own view is that there is an important difference between what lies behind an Act (the purpose) and what the Act lays down in order to achieve that purpose (why we are changing the law is different from changing the law) and that the former is normally better included, and is more likely to be formulated in a helpful way, in the Explanatory Notes rather than in the statute itself. So, e.g., a section in the Contracts (Rights of Third Parties) Act 1999 that the purpose of the Act was to reform the law on privity of contract so as to enable third parties in some situations to enforce contracts would have been odd in the statute itself but was helpfully included in the Explanatory Notes. That purpose clauses are better placed in the Explanatory Notes was also the view taken in the Norton Committee Report, at paras. 82–87. It should be added that although, applying a purposive interpretation, courts need to ascertain the statutory purpose, it is open to question how helpful, on a specific issue of statutory interpretation, the purpose set out in advance can be, whether in the statute or in the Explanatory Notes. Indeed, there is a danger that such a statement of purpose would simply degenerate in practice into an unhelpful factual list (adding nothing to the long title) or into a political manifesto.

a statute[30] and, in so far as it is thought inappropriate to include examples in the statute itself – and we could have a debate about that[31] – the Explanatory Notes now provide an obvious and uncontroversial place for them.

The benefit of examples has been particularly brought home to me in recent work I have been doing on the Myanmar Contract Act 1872, which is in all substantive respects identical to the Indian Contract Act 1872. That Act, brilliantly drafted by Sir James Fitzjames Stephen, sought to codify the general law of contract for India and other parts of the British Empire. A feature of it is that there is what are labelled 'illustrations' given throughout of how the provisions are seen as applying. This helps enormously in understanding the Act and in bringing it alive.

I now move on to Part 2 of this lecture, which looks more generally at the central role played by Parliamentary Counsel.

2 The Central Role of Parliamentary Counsel

Parliamentary Counsel are our drafting experts. While secondary legislation is drafted in Departments, Parliamentary

---

[30] *R (Westminster City Council)* v. *National Asylum Support Service* [2002] UKHL 38, [2002] 1 WLR 2956, per Lord Steyn; *Wilson* v. *First County Trust* (No 2) [2003] UKHL 40, [2004] 1 AC 816 at [64] (per Lord Nicholls).

[31] In Australia, there are statutory provisions which deal with how exactly one interprets examples in legislation: see, e.g., s. 36A(1) Interpretation Act 1984 (Vic) and s. 15(AD) Acts Interpretation Act 1901 (Cth).

Counsel draft almost all statutes in this jurisdiction.[32] Their role is therefore of great importance to us all. Yet few lawyers, let alone members of the public, will have ever met a Parliamentary Counsel or have any knowledge or real understanding of what they do.[33]

So I first encountered Parliamentary Counsel when I went to the Law Commission in 1994. At that time, there were five to six Parliamentary Counsel working at the Law Commission, most of whom were seconded from the Office of Parliamentary Counsel (OPC).[34] Some were working on law reform projects while others were working on consolidation or statute repeal bills. From the perspective of law reform, it was of huge benefit to have Parliamentary Counsel in our building because the drafting of the bill was of central importance in working out whether the policy would stand up or needed revision. At a certain point, there is a symbiotic relationship between the two as one refines the policy in the light of the drafting.[35] Although some Parliamentary Counsel had

---

[32] In practice, they draft all 'public general Acts' (i.e. all government bills and all private members' bills likely to pass) but they do not usually draft 'local Acts'. For the difference between 'public general Acts' and 'local Acts', see lecture 1, note 5.

[33] The Office of Parliamentary Counsel was set up in 1869. Prior to that, Acts were generally farmed out to barristers in private practice to draft. It would appear that a desire for consistency in drafting, as well, no doubt, as saving some money, led to the creation of the office.

[34] Although at least one had recently retired and was working part-time at the Commission.

[35] As Sir Geoffrey Palmer expressed it in his superb article, 'The Law Reform Enterprise: Evaluating the Past and Charting the Future' (2015) 131 *Law Quarterly Review* 402 at 413–414, 'No policy proposal can be

the reputation for being difficult, I found them all great to work with and I learned a huge amount from them.

There are four points I would like to make about the work of Parliamentary Counsel as I observed it.

(i) Even though in the same building, they required formal instructions from us in which we set out in detail what it was that we wanted. At that initial stage, they did not want us to give drafting suggestions and we were told off if we did so. We were supplying the policy. It was for them to turn it into a draft and not for us to draft for them.

(ii) On their receipt of the instructions, within a few days there would invariably be a response calling for clarification. This challenging function could go on for some time and was enormously valuable. Here were experienced rigorously analytical lawyers telling you that you had either not thought things through sufficiently clearly or, if you had, that what you were asking for would not work. So for example on the Contracts (Rights of Third Parties) Bill, concerned to allow third parties to enforce contracts, I recall being asked almost immediately for further information because we had not set out in the instructions what was meant by 'contract', by 'parties' and by 'enforcement'.

(iii) Once Counsel were satisfied that they had been given a clear and coherent policy, they would then draft fairly

properly understood and tested unless there is a bill drafted by parliamentary counsel. Embedding parliamentary counsel in the Commission in London was a stroke of genius.'

quickly and there would be helpful exchanges with us as they did so. Our comments on draft clauses were welcomed, and at this stage there was no objection to our suggesting preferred drafts of particular clauses. I came to appreciate, with great admiration, what Counsel could achieve. Sometimes, the initial drafts did not fully capture what we wanted or did so inelegantly. Almost always, Counsel would come back with a better form of words, even though we would never have thought of that linguistic solution ourselves.

(iv) Parliamentary Counsel often worked under considerable time pressure. Although this did not apply so much to Law Commission bills, where the timetable was relaxed, they were also sometimes drafting mainstream government bills while at the Commission. I recall finding in the photocopier at the Law Commission a document in which Parliamentary Counsel had been responding to a government department in relation to a bill. The document started with words to this effect: 'Much of the policy on this bill has not been properly worked out. I have been asked to draft a bill within 24 hours. The consequence is that, in the draft which you have, I have had to make up much of the policy myself.'

It should be clear from this that Parliamentary Counsel play a vital central role in law-making in our system and that the skills that they have cannot be quickly learned.[36] As former

---

[36] Elizabeth Gardiner, First Parliamentary Counsel, has told me that it takes about five to seven years to train a drafter to lead on a medium-sized bill (and those recruited are already solicitors or barristers with

Parliamentary Counsel Daniel Greenberg has expressed it in his book, *Laying Down the Law*:

> Parliamentary Counsel are in one sense the principal influence on and control over the precise wording of Acts of Parliament . . . I estimate that well in excess of 99 per cent of the words of the statute book not only are chosen by Counsel but are not seriously questioned or tested by anyone else before enactment.[37]

It is therefore welcome news that, after a difficult period from 2010, when the number of senior drafters at the OPC was reduced[38] (as part of a general move to reduce the numbers of highly paid senior civil servants)[39] and there were restrictions on public sector recruitment, there have been recruitment exercises for new drafters in 2014 and 2016, recruiting 15 new counsel.[40] This does tend to indicate that, however short-sighted it was to have lost some of the most experienced drafters from the top of the office, government has woken up to the fact that highly

---

some years of experience). She also tells me that, as a drafter, one is always learning. It follows that the most senior drafters have enormous expertise.

[37] Daniel Greenberg, *Laying Down the Law* (Sweet & Maxwell, 2011) 32–33.

[38] Ibid. at 23.

[39] Some in the Press dubbed the highly paid civil servants, which included some senior Parliamentary Counsel, as the civil service 'fat-cats'.

[40] Confining oneself to drafters working on the Government's legislative programme (i.e. excluding drafters seconded to the Law Commission or to the Tax Law Rewrite), there were around 25 drafters at the OPC in the 1980s, between 24 and 31 in the 1990s, and with a peak in 2010 of 57. As at December 2017, there are now 49. I am grateful to Elizabeth Gardiner for these figures.

skilled professional drafters are a necessity not a luxury. Brexit may well have helped in this regard.

However, and without wishing in any way to denigrate the efforts that have already been made, it is I think important that, to counter the sort of cut-backs that have occurred in the recent past, the profile of Parliamentary Counsel is raised so that Parliamentarians, and indeed the general public, are aware of the central importance of the role they perform. I am also conscious that, for example, much more could be done in the law schools in educating our students about the role of Parliamentary Counsel.

There are three final linked points about the role of Parliamentary Counsel that I would like to stress.

The first is that, while the quality of our legislation depends on both drafting and policy, from a drafter's perspective everything hinges on the quality of their instructions and hence on the clarity of the policy. As Elizabeth Gardiner, First Parliamentary Counsel, has stressed to me, if we are seeking to improve statutes, the single biggest factor is for Departments to ensure that the policy has been rigorously thought-through. Parliamentary Counsel cannot draft properly if the policy is unformulated and unclear.

Secondly, I have indicated already that an important function of Parliamentary Counsel is in challenging the instructions given to them. At the Law Commission, I found this almost as important as the drafting itself. It is imperative that this challenging role is not diminished. An important check on government officials will be lost if the status and role of Parliamentary Counsel, and their ability to challenge policy on technical grounds, is in any way diminished.[41]

Daniel Greenberg recounts in his book *Laying Down the Law*[42] that so important did he consider this challenging role to be that 'when it became fashionable for government notepaper to carry meaningless slogans by way of self-congratulation at the top or bottom, for some time my letters went out with a small footer at the bottom saying "Parliamentary Counsel – we aim to displease"'.

Thirdly, Parliamentary Counsel should, so far as possible, resist the pressure to allow statutes to be used for purposes other than changing the law. In my experience at the Law Commission, Parliamentary Counsel were very reluctant to draft declaratory provisions – that is, provisions which, for the avoidance of doubt, simply state what the existing law is – even though on at least one project I thought such clauses could be very useful. I was told, 'You are either changing the law or you are not. If you are not, leave well alone.' Another former Parliamentary Counsel put it more starkly: 'I operated a shoot to kill policy for anyone who asked for a declaratory provision.' Although I found it really frustrating at the time, I now accept that this was, and is, the correct approach.[43] Apart from wasting valuable time in a crowded

---

[41] See Sir Geoffrey Bowman, 'Why Do We Have an Office of Parliamentary Counsel?' (2005) 26 *Statute Law Review* 69, 70–73, 81; Daniel Greenberg, *Laying Down the Law* (Sweet & Maxwell, 2011) 23–24, 32.

[42] Greenberg, *Laying Down the Law* at 32.

[43] See Daniel Greenberg, *Craies on Legislation* (11th edn, Sweet & Maxwell, 2017) 73–79 and paras. 8.1.12–8.1.13. For the classic judicial statement on

legislative timetable, as well as adding to the length and complexity of the statute book, declaratory provisions may cause needless confusion because inevitably those affected, and in turn the courts, are anxious to ascertain whether such provisions have changed the law or not. They may tend to the view that such a legislative provision is most unlikely to have been included unless the existing law was in doubt or unclear even though that may not be so. Nevertheless, there are many declaratory provisions in our statutes. A Westlaw search I recently conducted indicated that there were well over 1,000. Some of these are even more problematic because they are plainly designed to make a political, rather than a legal, point. Good examples[44] are section 1 of both the Compensation Act 2006 and the Social Action, Responsibility and Heroism Act 2015, which require courts, when deciding whether a person has met a standard of care for the purpose of an action in negligence or breach of statutory duty, to have regard to whether the defendant was acting for the benefit of society, or volunteering, or acting

the problems that may be caused by declaratory provisions, see *McLaughlin* v. *Westgarth* (1906) 75 LJPC 117, 118 (per Lord Halsbury). For consideration of whether particular statutes were merely declaratory of the common law doctrine of 'acts of a de facto officer' (as applied to a judge), see *Adams* v. *Adams* [1971] P 188; *Fawdry & Co* v. *Murfitt* [2002] EWCA Civ 643, [2003] 4 All ER 60 at [18]–[30].

[44] Similarly Daniel Greenberg has argued that s. 1 of the National Citizens Services Act 2017, setting up a corporate body, could have been equally well achieved without legislation: see Constitution Committee's 2017 Report on *Preparing Legislation*, paras. 10–11. But it is not clear that the relevant funding and auditing arrangements could have been achieved without the body being set up by statute.

heroically for someone else's benefit. But this was already the position at common law.[45] Somewhat similar and equally to be deplored are statutes, labelled 'aspirational legislation'[46] by Professor David Feldman, which, while not declaratory, set out policy aspirations rather than changing the law. Policy aspirations are no doubt politically important but the appropriate home for them is elsewhere as, for example, in a Ministerial statement to Parliament. My message on this third point therefore is simple: Parliamentary Counsel should, if at all possible, resist the pressure to draft declaratory and aspirational statutory provisions.

3 The Role of the Law Commission in Respect of Consolidation and Statute Law Repeals

Although the principal role of the Law Commission is to recommend law reform, it should not be overlooked that

---

[45] See, e.g., *Scout Association* v. *Barnes* [2010] EWCA Civ 1476 at 34.

[46] 'Legislation which Bears no Law' (2016) 37 *Statute Law Review* 212, 220. As examples, Feldman refers to s. 1 of the Climate Change Act 2008 and the short-lived Fiscal Responsibility Act 2010. Closely related to this (I am grateful for this point and example to Professor Charles Mitchell of UCL) is that care must be taken to ensure that a politically motivated statutory 'change' to the common law is based on a correct understanding of the common law: what is now s. 4(2) Charities Act 2011 might be said to fall foul of this because it would seem that the supposed 'presumption' of public benefit that that subsection appeared to remove did not exist at common law. See *Independent Schools Council* v. *Charity Commission for England and Wales* [2011] UKUT 421 (TCC), [2012] Ch 214 at [41]-[93]; Alison Dunn, 'Using the Wrong Policy Tools: Education, Charity, and Public Benefit' (2012) 39 *Journal of Law and Society* 491, esp. 508-509.

included within its work, as laid down in section 3(1) of the Law Commissions Act 1965, is the consolidation of statutes and statute law repeals.[47] Although perhaps less glamorous than law reform (although some might consider, I know not, that even law reform is not that sexy a topic), the importance of this work should not be underestimated.[48]

Consolidation refers to where there are several statutes dealing with the same subject area, usually piled one upon another at different dates, and the aim of consolidation is to bring them all within one (or occasionally more than one) self-contained well-structured statute, which makes matters so much easier for the user of the statutes[49] and is one way in which the statute book can be kept in some sort of

---

[47] There is a special expedited procedure in Parliament for consolidation and statute law revision bills that go to a joint select committee of both Houses (the Consolidation Bills Joint Committee). See generally Michael Zander, *The Law-Making Process* (7th edn, Hart, 2015) 58–61. Prior to this work being undertaken by the Law Commission on its creation in 1965, the work fell within the remit of the Statute Law Committee, which was set up in 1868 and chaired by the Lord Chancellor. Its membership initially comprised civil servants, MPs, First Parliamentary Counsel and the equivalent in Scotland, but, after 1945, its membership was increased to include law officers and Law Lords.

[48] George Gretton, 'The Duty to Make the Law More Accessible? The Two C-Words' in *Fifty Years of the Law Commissions* (eds. Matt Dyson, James Lee and Shona Wilson Stark, Hart, 2016) 89, 92–93.

[49] It might be thought that consolidation is a relatively mechanical task but there is scope for reordering and there may need to be minor amendments, sometimes secured in advance of the consolidation, so as to ensure that the consolidation Act can be a single and coherent piece of legislation.

good order.[50] The work of consolidation has always involved Parliamentary Counsel and that was the core work of two of the Parliamentary Counsel seconded to the Law Commission during my years there.

It is important to clarify that the principal purpose of consolidation is not to ensure that subsequent amendments to an Act can easily be seen. Whatever the position in the past, this is no longer a significant problem because the vast majority of amendments are made by 'textual amendment'[51] and the electronic versions of statutes provided commercially by Westlaw or Lexis – or, although not fully up-to-date, the free website at legislation.gov.uk – include subsequent textual amendments so that we can straightforwardly see how a principal Act looks as amended.

I interject here to say how shocking it is that there is still no fully up-to-date free website of primary (let alone secondary) UK legislation so that if you want to find out

---

[50] The Renton Committee Report in 1975 paras. 13.23 and 14.3 said that, according to the rough estimate of First Parliamentary Counsel, there were about 8,000 pages of Acts that were in need of consolidation.

[51] This means that the amending Act sets out the words (usually in inverted commas) that are to be inserted or deleted in the other Act, and where the insertions and deletions are to be made. This contrasts with the older technique of 'non-textual amendment' whereby the amendment to another Act is described without setting out directly the words in the other Act that are to be inserted or deleted so that the amendments do not become part of the earlier statute. For an example of the two techniques, see the Renton Committee Report para. 13.3. For an excellent relatively recent example of non-textual amendment, see the Contracts (Rights of Third Parties) Act 1999, s. 7(2)–(3).

accurately today what the statute law is in any area you have to pay Westlaw or Lexis for that privilege.

Therefore, rather than ease in seeing amendments, the principal purpose of consolidation is to overcome the problem of there being more than one statute in the same area possibly with different structures and possibly applying at different points in time. A classic example is the law on criminal sentences where, in recent years, there have been many statutes laying down new sentences with complex commencement and transitional provisions. But there are many other areas that today would also benefit from consolidation, such as the law on defamation, financial services, immigration, pensions, and family law.

So what work has the Law Commission recently been doing on consolidation? At least at first sight, the answer is alarming. Between its establishment in 1965 and 2006, the Law Commission was responsible for 220 consolidation Acts. Since 2006, there have only been two.[52] This is essentially down to resources[53] (although there have been frustrations

---

[52] The Charities Act 2011 and the Co-operative and Community Benefit Societies Act 2014.

[53] See the Law Commission Annual Report (2016–2017) p. 54: '[I]n a time of reduced funding in most areas of public services and, specifically, reduced core funding for the Law Commission, consolidation on the old-fashioned model can no longer be considered a priority. However, the need for simplification of the law is as great as it ever has been. The pattern in future is likely to be codification rather than a simple consolidation in areas where statute law is incoherent or confusing and where codification would bring genuine practical benefits.' See also the Law Commission Annual Report (2012–2013) para. 2.125: 'We are mindful that consolidation is one of our statutory functions, and we

where consolidation bills have been ready to be enacted only for new reforms then to be put forward). Although the Law Commission may be paid additionally by particular Departments for so-called 'references', the core funding for the Law Commission from the Ministry of Justice has been severely cut back in recent years. So between 2010 and 2015, the core funding was cut from approximately £4 M to £3 M and the present target appears to be to cut this to £2 M by 2020.[54] This links to the fact that Parliamentary Counsel are essential to consolidation work and, as we have seen, the OPC has itself suffered cut-backs. In prioritising its work, the Law Commission has therefore been forced to recognise that, with some specific limited exceptions, consolidation work cannot be undertaken.[55]

It is worth dwelling just for a moment on the main specific exception, which is the Law Commission's sentencing project.[56] Although there is some technical reform to

remain of the view that consolidation is a valuable contribution to improving the state of the statute book. We welcome any encouragement that can be given to Departments to see consolidation as a higher priority than now seems to be the case, and we always do our best to encourage it ourselves.' See also the Law Commission Annual Report (2010–2011) para. 2.83 which explains the waste of four years' work on the consolidation of the legislation on private pensions when the relevant Department withdrew its support.

[54] See the evidence given by Lord Justice Bean, Chair of the Law Commission, to the House of Lords Constitution Committee (21 December 2016).

[55] See, especially, the Law Commission Annual Report (2010–2011) para. 2.85.

[56] A Consultation paper *The Sentencing Code* with draft bill was published on 27 July 2017.

overcome timing issues – the so-called 'clean sweep' – this is essentially a consolidation project, and it beautifully illustrates the importance of consolidation. So the aim is to produce a single sentencing statute, referred to by the Law Commission as a sentencing code, to replace the myriad of complex and overlapping statutes that we now have. The present law is so difficult to find and understand that, in a random survey of 262 cases reaching the Court of Appeal (Criminal Division), it was found that in over a third the judge had mistakenly passed an unlawful sentence.[57] Apart from the injustice being caused, the cost of this in terms of, for example, wasted court time is enormous and dwarfs many times over the annual budget of the Law Commission.[58]

It is therefore clear that if we want the Law Commission to carry out the consolidation work that was entrusted to it in its founding statute, it must be given the funding needed, which includes the cost of Parliamentary Counsel who are essential to consolidation work. To bring this about, Parliamentarians and Departments need to be made aware of why this work matters.[59] And it matters

---

[57] *The Sentencing Code,* Consultation Paper Summary, para. 1.10. These were not cases where the sentence was manifestly excessive or unduly lenient but ones in which the type of sentence imposed was simply wrong in law.

[58] Ibid. at para. 1.28.

[59] It is also essential that Parliamentarians and Departments understand that, once there has been consolidation, subsequent reforms should be consistent with the consolidated statute. The good work of consolidation will be diminished if there is ill-discipline in respect of subsequent reforms to that consolidated statute. This is a point made forcibly by the Law Commission in *The Sentencing Code,* Consultation Paper No. 232

because if the statute book is out of control so that even judges cannot easily find the applicable law and are making basic mistakes, this is not only contrary to the rule of law but is potentially very costly. It is therefore very welcome news that the House of Lords Constitution Committee's 2017 Report on *Preparing Legislation* recommended that 'Government should, as a priority, provide the Law Commission with the necessary resources to start consolidating those areas of the law where consistent application of the law is now under threat from the sheer complexity of the existing statute book.'[60] All pressure should now be brought to bear on the Ministry of Justice and presumably the Treasury to accept and act on that recommendation of the House of Lords Constitution Committee.

But what about the Law Commission's work on statute law repeals, which was not touched on at all in that recent report? Although statute law repeals is like consolidation in that it seeks to keep the statute book under some sort of control the work is very different from consolidation because it is concerned with the repeal of obsolete statutes. It only

(2017), paras. 1.20, 1.45, 3.86–3.89. So at para. 1.45 it is said: 'Previous attempts at the consolidation of sentencing law, such as the Powers of Criminal Courts (Sentencing) Act 2000, have been frustrated by being rapidly overtaken by other legislation. While this paper is subject to consultation we will be working closely with Parliamentary stakeholders, and those responsible for the drafting of legislation, to emphasise the benefits of the Sentencing Code remaining the main source of legislative sentencing material, and that amendments should be enacted in a way that retains the benefit of our new approach to transitional arrangements.'

[60] Constitution Committee's 2017 Report on *Preparing Legislation*, paras. 133–147.

serves to confuse if statutes that have outlived any realistic purpose are left on the statute book. But, of course, one has to be very careful not to repeal a statute that might still have some use. This is highly skilled work which involves both painstaking enquiries and historical understanding. Between 1965 and 2013, the Law Commission's work led to over 3,000 statutes being repealed in their entirety and the partial repeal of thousands of others.[61] Yet now the government appears to have lost interest in this type of work. The latest (20th) Law Commission Statute Law Repeals Report in 2015, with a draft statute law repeals bill attached, was expected to be implemented in 2016 but instead it has simply being gathering dust in the Ministry of Justice even though there is a very quick expedited Parliamentary procedure for implementation of statutory repeal bills. The report recommends the repeal of over 200 obsolete statutes, in whole or in part (the oldest being an Act in 1267 and the most recent being an Act in 2007).[62] It is hard to see any good reason why that report has not been implemented. Moreover, without interest from government, and again because of the need to prioritise in the light of reduced funding, as I understand it no statute law repeal

---

[61] See the Law Commission's Annual Report (2016–2017) at p. 54. As my focus in these lectures is on 'public general Acts' and not 'local Acts' (see above Lecture 1 note 5), I should clarify that many of the statutes that have been repealed have been local, and not public general, Acts.

[62] The recommended repeals cover a wide range of topics from agriculture and churches to trade and industry and taxation. The earliest recommended repeal is from the Statute of Marlborough 1267. Passed during the reign of Henry III, the Statute is one of the oldest surviving pieces of legislation. The most recent recommended repeal is part of the Consumers, Estate Agents and Redress Act 2007.

work is being carried out or is planned to be carried out by the Law Commission. Again Parliamentarians and Departments have to be made aware of why this work matters and the necessary funding, and Departmental support, should be given to the Law Commission so that this often overlooked, but important work, can be recommenced.[63]

This leads directly to a more general question about the age of statutes. The default position is that a statute lasts indefinitely.[64] Inevitably, therefore, statutes become out of date even though they remain on the statute book. Moreover, given that it is so much easier to enact than to repeal, this is a continuing and ever-growing problem. One response to it is the statute repeal work entrusted to the Law Commission. Another is to insert into the statute a time limitation thereby overriding the default position. So, for example, 'sunset clauses' by which statutes lapse unless renewed after a period of time are sometimes used especially for controversial statutes. It can be powerfully argued that far greater use should be made of sunset clauses, or other time restrictions, so as to minimise the problem of ageing statutes.[65]

---

[63] If those funds are not forthcoming, it would be worth exploring whether the Law Commission might enlist the help of academics, most obviously legal historians, funded by research grants.

[64] As is said in Daniel Greenberg, *Craies on Legislation* (11th edn, Sweet & Maxwell, 2017), para. 10.2.2, 'an Act could lie dormant for a number of years, even for centuries, and still be available for use.' It is there suggested that, using a very old statute without warning, could now potentially be an infringement of the Human Rights Act 1998.

[65] Some statutes especially in wartime are even named as temporary; and there are other even very well-known statutes that only last a fixed period

Focussing on obsolete statutes brings me back to Professor Guido Calabresi's book *A Common Law for the Age of Statutes*,[66] which I referred to in the first sentence of my first lecture. Calabresi recognised that, because it is so much easier to enact than to repeal statutes, out-of-date statutes were a continuing and ever-growing problem. His proposal for dealing with the age of statutes – and hence the title of his book – was that the courts, using standard common law technique, should simply themselves update statutes just as they update the common law. In my first lecture, I drew a fundamental distinction between legitimate judicial inter-pretation and illegitimate judicial legislation: although the former permits a purposive up-to-date interpretation of a statute, the meaning given must be a plausible meaning of the words used in the statute so that, for example, a statute applying to dogs cannot be applied to cats even if the judges consider that the statutory purpose embraces both.[67] But there is no such linguistic constraint in Calabresi's approach so that the courts would simply be free to extend the statute to cats as well as dogs. In my view, his approach crosses the line to judicial legislation and is plainly constitutionally unacceptable.

---

of time, e.g., income tax is an annual tax so that s. 1 of the annual Finance Act imposes the charge to income tax only for the tax year in question.

[66] Guido Calabresi, *A Common Law for the Age of Statutes* (Harvard University Press, 1982). The title is often cited without full appreciation of his thesis, which was a play on the words 'the age of statutes' (the 'era' of statutes' and the 'old-age' of statutes).

[67] Above at p. 43.

4 Pre- and Post-Legislative Scrutiny

Pre-Legislative Scrutiny

Over the last twenty years or so, an important development, designed to improve the quality of statutes, has been the increased emphasis on pre-legislative scrutiny (commonly known as 'PLS'). This refers to the publication of draft bills (or draft clauses) for consideration, particularly by Parliamentary Committees, prior to Parliament formally starting to consider the bill on first reading.[68] This pre-

---

[68] In theory, pre-legislative scrutiny need not involve a Parliamentary Committee. But the vast majority of those draft bills that are published are scrutinised by a parliamentary committee. This may be a joint committee of both Houses set up specifically to consider the draft bill (e.g. the Joint Committee on the Draft Investigatory Powers Bill). But there are standing select committees that are often used for this purpose, e.g., the Joint Committee on Human Rights, the House of Commons Justice Committee, the House of Commons Home Affairs Committee, the House of Lords Constitution Committee, and the House of Lords Delegated Powers and Regulatory Reform Committee. There may also be a particularly appropriate standing committee for the area in question (e.g. the Welsh Affairs Select Committee considered the Draft Wales Bill). Closely linked to PLS is the publication of green and white papers without a draft bill or draft clauses: such a consultation process helps to refine policy and is therefore to be welcomed (see Constitution Committee's 2017 Report on *Preparing Legislation* paras. 38–42) but, as the devil is often in the detail of legislation (and, as has been said above at p. 101, there is a symbiotic interplay between drafting and policy), additional consultation on a draft bill is likely to be even more beneficial. The Law Commission consults widely on its recommendations and the final Report usually includes publication of a draft bill that is directly influenced by that consultation process: but the draft bill itself is not usually consulted on by the Law Commission, although the Government

legislative stage enables a wide range of views to be considered, not least from experts in the area and from those directly affected, at a stage when, very importantly, one can see what the provisions of the Act will look like and yet there is still a good prospect of proposed amendments being accepted prior to the government's position becoming entrenched. While PLS adds extra time to the process (including additional drafting time by Parliamentary Counsel),[69] the additional opportunity for reflection and informed comment is very likely to improve the end product.[70] As one

may itself undertake pre-legislative scrutiny of the Law Commission's draft bill (with or without modifications).

[69] In his lecture to the Statute Law Society on 28 February 2017 entitled 'Why Is There So Much Bad Legislation?', Lord Lisvane said that, as a rough generalisation, he understood from Parliamentary Counsel that PLS on a bill added 50% drafting time.

[70] Cabinet Office's *Guide to Making Legislation* (2015) at para. 22.4 states: 'There are a number of reasons why publication in draft for pre-legislative scrutiny is desirable. It allows thorough consultation on the bill while it is still in a more easily amendable form, and makes it easier to ensure that both potential parliamentary objections and stakeholder views are elicited. This can assist the passage of the bill when it is introduced to parliament at a later stage and increases scrutiny of government legislation.' In summary, PLS may be expected to lead to better legislation for at least three reasons. First, it enables people outside Parliament, especially those most affected and experts in the area, to examine what the Act will look like. Secondly, there is an enhanced prospect through this process of influencing the government before the policy is set in stone. Thirdly, precisely because one has the bill in advance, needless uncertainty or complexity in the drafting can be eradicated. PLS seems such a beneficial step forward that one wonders why it took so long to be accepted. The Hansard Society, *Making the Law* (1992), pp. 35–37, which recommended this innovation, indicated that

commentator has put it, 'This may not be a perfect cure to Parliament's tendency to legislate in haste and repeal at leisure but it is a significant development in the way laws are made.'[71] And there have been several studies showing the beneficial impact that pre-legislative scrutiny has had on particular bills which have included both drafting and policy changes.[72]

Perhaps not surprisingly, therefore, the official stated view, as set out in the Cabinet Office's *Guide to Making Legislation*, is that PLS is the default position so that, if

opposition to it appeared to rest on the misapprehension that it was constitutionally improper to disclose the details of a bill prior to its formal introduction in Parliament. PLS was further fervently endorsed by the Norton Committee Report in 2004. A further linked suggestion made in the Norton Committee Report – strongly endorsed by the Constitution Committee's 2017 Report on *Preparing Legislation* at paras. 177–182, which also recommended the creation of a legislative standards committee – is that PLS could be further enhanced by the introduction of scrutiny standards and checklists. See also Dawn Oliver, 'Improving the Scrutiny of Bills: the Case for Standards and Checklists' (2006) *Public Law* 219.

[71] A. Kennon, 'Pre-Legislative Scrutiny of Draft Bills' (2004) *Public Law* 477, 477.

[72] Ibid.; J. Smookler, 'Making a Difference? The Effectiveness of Pre-Legislative Scrutiny' (2006) 59 *Parliamentary Affairs* 522; Andrew Le Sueur and Jack Caird, 'The House of Lords Select Committee on the Constitution' in *Parliament and the Law* (eds. A. Horne, G. Drewry and D. Oliver, Hart, 2013) 289–299 (which looked at the impact of the Constitution Committee on the Legislative and Regulatory Reform Bill 2006 and the Health and Social Care Bill 2011, prior to and during the passage of those bills). In one case, even the title of the bill was amended after PLS: the Mental Incapacity Bill was amended to the Mental Capacity Bill.

a draft bill is not going to be published, the Department must have a good reason for not doing so.[73]

In practice, however, this is not what is happening.[74] Of the bills that became the 71 Acts passed in the last two Parliamentary sessions – 2015–2016 and 2016–2017 – it would appear[75] that, leaving aside draft finance bills, PLS was used in relation to only two, i.e. the Investigatory Powers Act 2016 and the Wales Act 2017.[76] Of course, there will be bills where pre-

---

[73] (2017) at para. 22.1: 'The default position should be that bills will be published in draft prior to formal introduction. There should be a good reason not to publish the bill in draft. The Government is committed to publishing more of its bills in draft before they are formally introduced to Parliament, and to submitting them to a parliamentary committee for parliamentary pre-legislative scrutiny where possible.'

[74] Although writing in 2012, in the words of Murray Hunt, 'The Joint Committee on Human Rights' in *Parliament and the Law* (eds. A. Horne, G. Drewry and D. Oliver, Hart, 2013) at 233, 'most government bills are still not published as draft bills first'.

[75] As the next footnote indicates, I have here relied on published information. It may be that there is some additional informal PLS, not least where opinions are sought on one clause of a bill or a few clauses only, that is not reflected in that published information.

[76] See *Pre-Legislative Scrutiny under the 2015 and 2017 Conservative Governments,* House of Commons Library Briefing Paper, CBP-7757, 19 September 2017; and the Parliament website. Draft bills were also produced in respect of energy, spaceflight, and a public services ombudsman; and, in respect of the first two of these, there are now (in the present session 2017–2019) two bills, the Smart Meters Bill and the Space Industry Bill. In the present session (2017–2019), there have also been four draft bills published on tariff caps for domestic gas and electricity, on health service safety investigations, on tenants' fees, and on animal welfare. Although not listed under the draft bills section of the Parliament website, the Government has also published draft personal injury discount legislation and there was pre-legislative scrutiny of that

legislative scrutiny is inappropriate.[77] But, in general, every effort should be made to ensure that, in practice, PLS is the norm and that the officially stated enthusiasm for it does not drift backwards. I therefore welcome the recommendation in the House of Lords Constitution Committee's 2017 Report on *Preparing Legislation* that PLS should *not* be treated as 'an optional extra ... [but] should be considered an integral part of the ... legislative process'.[78]

by the Justice Committee: see its Report dated 20 November 2017 available on the Parliament website. Appendix 4 Table 1 of the Briefing Paper, CBP-7757, shows that 35 draft bills or substantial sets of clauses (excluding draft finance bills) were published by the Government in the 2010–2015 Parliament; and in the three Parliaments between 1997 and 2010, 75 draft bills or substantial sets of clauses were published (17 in the 1997 Parliament; 33 in the 2001 Parliament; and 25 in the 2005 Parliament). That table also shows that slightly more draft bills were published than were scrutinised by committee (the numbers in the last sentence refer to the draft bills published). In the last two Parliamentary sessions, there were five Acts implementing Law Commission bills in whole or part: Charities (Protection and Social Investment) Act 2016, Enterprise Act 2016 (Part 5), Policing and Crime Act 2017 (Part 6), Intellectual Property (Unjustified Threats) Act 2017, Digital Economy Act 2017. But it would appear that none of those bills was subject to pre-legislative scrutiny (although clearly the bills were directly influenced by the Law Commission's consultation process and there may have been informal PLS of the type mentioned in the previous footnote).

[77] E.g. bills that are needed to meet international commitments where there is little flexibility around implementation, bills to implement budget commitments, or bills which must reach the statute book quickly due to pressing need: see Cabinet Office's *Guide to Making Legislation* (2017) at para. 22.

[78] Constitution Committee's 2017 Report on *Preparing Legislation* at para. 87. It was suggested that one way of integrating PLS more fully into the

Post-Legislative Scrutiny

If the case for pre-legislative scrutiny seems obvious, one might have thought it was even more clear-cut that everyone involved can learn an enormous amount by considering ex post facto how well a statute has fared. How can it be sensible to plough on with new legislation when we are not learning, for good or ill, from what has happened in the past? The Law Commission in 2006 recommended that, in order to ensure systematic post-legislative scrutiny, consideration should be given to setting up a new Parliamentary Joint Committee for Post-Legislative Scrutiny.[79] Disappointingly, in 2008 the government did not agree with that suggestion, although it did accept that Departments should generally produce a memorandum, within three to five years of Royal Assent, on the post-legislative review of an Act, which the relevant select committee could then take further in a full review.[80] And this is the official approach embodied in the Cabinet Office's *Guide to Making Legislation*.[81]

process would be to adjust the time subsequently needed for passage of a bill where there has been PLS.

[79] *Post-Legislative Scrutiny*, Law Com Report No 302 (2006). This followed the Law Commission's Consultation Paper No 178.

[80] Office of the Leader of the House of Commons, *Post-Legislative Scrutiny – The Government's Approach* March 2008, Cm 7320.

[81] At chapter 43: 'Three to five years (normally) after Royal Assent, the responsible department must submit a memorandum to the relevant Commons departmental select committee (unless it has been agreed with the committee that a memorandum is not required), published as a command paper.' At para. 43.13: 'Non-submission of a memorandum would be the exception and the department will need to make its case to the committee, and inform the PBL Secretariat of its intention to do so.'

Unfortunately, as with pre-legislative scrutiny, the official line on post-legislative scrutiny is not being adhered to in practice. Although pinning down what has been happening is not easy, there is a helpful Commons Library Note which points out that in the Commons between May 2010 and January 2013, while there were 58 post-legislative memoranda, only three of those had been the subject of reports by select committees.[82] And while in 2011 the House of Lords Liaison Committee took on an active role in relation to post-legislative scrutiny that appears to have resulted in only six post-legislative reports by a Lords ad hoc select committee in the six years since.[83] The position appears to

At para. 43.2, there is a helpful summary of what are seen to be the advantages of systematic post-legislative scrutiny: they include, 'Allowing lessons (both about what has worked well and what has not worked well) to be learnt and disseminated to the benefit of other legislation.' At the same time, the need for a proportionate approach is stressed: one clearly cannot devote excessive time to looking back at the expense of moving forward. So para. 43.3 reads: 'At the same time, the intention is to ensure that such scrutiny is proportionate to need. In particular, it is not envisaged that there should be a full in-depth review of every Act.'

[82] *Post-Legislative Scrutiny,* House of Commons Library Note SN/PC/05232 (last updated 23 May 2013). That Library Note also pointed out that there had been, in addition, some post-legislative reviews by committees not prompted by post-legislative memoranda (e.g. the post-legislative reviews of the Gambling Act 2005 and the Parliamentary Standards Act 2009). It further pointed out that, as at May 2013, post-legislative scrutiny was being undertaken by Commons committees into the Mental Capacity Act 2005, the Charities Act 2006, and the Mental Health Act 2005.

[83] These have been on: adoption legislation, the Mental Capacity Act 2005, the Inquiries Act 2005, extradition legislation, the Equality Act 2010, and

remain, therefore, one of limited and non-systematic post-legislative scrutiny.[84]

Assuming that the government is not willing to revisit the Law Commission's 2006 suggestion of a Parliamentary joint committee on post-legislative scrutiny, what can be done to improve the position? One possibility might be to supplement the post-legislative scrutiny by Parliamentary committees and departments by enlisting the help of academics.[85] I have previously suggested that to escape from judging the success of the Law Commission's work solely by quantity – the rate of implementation of its recommendations – rather than by the more important criterion of quality, a post-legislative review of Law Commission-inspired statutes could usefully and appropriately be carried out by research-funded legal academics.[86] This idea could be extended to

the Licensing Act 2003. See the various reports of the House of Lords Liaison Committee.

[84] I put to one side that form of post-legislative scrutiny that is built into an Act because the Act has to be renewed after a period of time. An example was the control orders legislation that had to be renewed annually, otherwise it would lapse.

[85] For the Law Commission's consideration of the role of independent reviewers, see *Post-Legislative Scrutiny*, Law Commission Report No 302 (2006) paras. 3.49–3.54: but academic input is mentioned only at para. 3.42 in the context of providing independent research into a Parliamentary committee. For a suggestion that post-legislative work might be 'outsourced' to 'external independent institutions such as universities', see Franklin De Vrieze and Victoria Hasson, 'Post-Legislative Scrutiny' (Westminster Foundation for Democracy, 2017), para. 7.5.

[86] 'Post-legislative Scrutiny, Legislative Drafting and the "Elusive Boundary"' in *Fifty Years of the Law Commissions* (eds. Matt Dyson,

cover the post-legislative scrutiny of all statutes, not just those implementing Law Commission reports, with the ultimate aim of the lessons of the past being used to inform the statutes of the future.[87]

Conclusion

In this lecture, I have made four main suggestions, or series of suggestions, as to ways in which our statute law can be

James Lee and Shona Wilson Stark, Hart, 2016) 188, 190–191. See in the same volume the helpful observations on this proposal from the perspective of criminal law reform, by David Ormerod, 'Reflections on the Courts and the Commission' 326, 334–335. I also suggested that there were likely to be useful consequential spin-offs from this type of study. So another question about legislation that I have long pondered over is this: are clauses giving discretion to the courts better or worse than those which lay down clear rules or principles? To give a well-known concrete example, within the Limitation Act 1980, is section 33 better or worse than sections 2 and 5? Post-legislative scrutiny of Law Commission Acts can be expected to help to answer that type of question.

[87] Admittedly, robust criteria will need to be devised for assessing the success of a statute and this may not be easy but is, in my view, surmountable. At least from a lawyer's perspective, relevant factors will surely include the numbers of cases coming to court based on uncertainties in the Act, any judicial, academic, or other comments on the Act including its drafting, the extent to which those directly affected consider that the Act has dealt satisfactorily with the underlying mischief, the extent to which those affected by the Act or lawyers advising on it can easily understand it, whether there have been any unfortunate unintended consequences, and the extent to which amending legislation has proved necessary. Indeed, if we cannot devise criteria for assessing the success of an Act, it would seem to follow that we are incapable of forming an evidence-based view as to whether any law, whether judge-made or legislative, is good or bad.

improved. First, not least because of the modern move to purposive statutory interpretation, there is room for a shift of culture towards more principled drafting; and a greater use of examples would also be helpful. Secondly, the profile of the Office of Parliamentary Counsel, which is so central to the quality of our statutes, could beneficially be raised; and government officials should not only properly respect Parliamentary Counsel's challenging function but should also be made fully aware of why declaratory and aspirational provisions ought not be included in legislation. Thirdly, Parliamentarians and Departments need to know why statutory consolidation and statute law repeals matter with a view to restoring the necessary funding, and Departmental support, for the Law Commission to re-engage fully with that work as its founding statute lays down. Fourthly, pre-legislative scrutiny should not be allowed to drift backwards; and post-legislative scrutiny should be more commonly and systematically undertaken with consideration being given to whether academics might usefully be enlisted to help with that work.

I return to drafting. While at the Law Commission, I learned a huge amount about drafting from Sir Geoffrey Bowman who after his time seconded to the Law Commission became First Parliamentary Counsel. In 2005, he wrote a classic article entitled 'Why do we have an office of Parliamentary Counsel?'.[88] It is full of characteristic wit and

---

[88] (2005) 26 *Statute Law Review* 69. See also Daniel Greenberg, 'All Trains Stop at Crewe: The Rise and Rise of Contextual Drafting' (2005) 7 *European Journal of Law Reform* 31.

wisdom. It includes his worrying about a sign in a railway station that 'Passengers must cross by the subway' and his vision of a passenger feeling bound to cross whether he wanted to get to the other side or not and then that poor passenger's whole life spent crossing and re-crossing by the subway when he finds that there is the same notice on the other side. As Sir Geoffrey wrote, and as he indicated to me many times, 'That might give you some insight into the … mad world that legislative drafters inhabit.'

As this is the last lecture in this Hamlyn series, I would like, finally, to draw out the main themes of the three lectures. I can do so with three sets of brief concluding observations.

First, we need to spend far more time in our university law schools researching, and teaching in an engaging and practical way, about statute law as a coherent whole. It is simply not good enough, for example, for students to be given the impression that statutory interpretation revolves around the literal rule, the mischief rule and the golden rule and that otherwise they can pick it up by a process of osmosis. Studying statutes as a coherent whole also helps us to understand properly the many fascinating issues raised by the interaction between common law and statute.

Secondly, in both my first and second lectures much of the focus has been on the power of the judiciary as against the Legislature. While judicial law-making power through development of the common law has been widely recognised since the demise of the declaratory fairy tale, the power of the judiciary in respect of statutory interpretation remains obfuscated by the idea that the courts are simply effecting the intention of Parliament. That idea is unhelpful, at best, and tends to operate as a fiction or mask. It is unacceptable, as we strive for rational transparency, for the courts' true reasoning to be hidden in that way. At the same time, we should recognise that both in interpreting statutes and in developing the common law, the judges operate under institutional constraints, which render it misleading to think of them as unelected mini-legislators. In any event, in our system, Parliamentary sovereignty is the ultimate check on judicial power.

Thirdly, we have the statutes that we deserve. I have a vision of an up-to-date freely accessible electronic statute database with statutes that are as easy to understand as possible because the principles have been made clear and are enlivened by examples, that have been subject to pre-legislative scrutiny, that are consolidated where helpful, where there are no obsolete intruders, and where the lessons of the past have been learnt through systematic post-legislative scrutiny. But fulfilment of that vision requires both resources and education. And it starts with all of us, who care for the state of our law, thinking much more seriously than we have been doing about our statutes.

INDEX

For EU product safety concerns, contact us at Calle de José Abascal, 56–1°, 28003 Madrid, Spain or eugpsr@cambridge.org.